STATISTICS

Walker Maths Essentials: Statistics 4+
1st Edition
Charlotte Walker
Victoria Walker

Cover and text design: Cheryl Smith, Macarn Design
Production controller: Siew Han Ong

Any URLs contained in this publication were checked for currency during the production process. Note, however, that the publisher cannot vouch for the ongoing currency of URLs.

Acknowledgements
Cover photo courtesy of Shutterstock

The authors wish to thank past and present colleagues who have generously shared their expertise and ideas.

For product information and technology assistance,
in Australia call **1300 790 853**;
in New Zealand call **0800 449 725**

For permission to use material from this text or product, please email **aust.permissions@cengage.com**

National Library of New Zealand Cataloguing-in-Publication Data
A catalogue record for this book is available from the National Library of New Zealand

978 01 7045142 0

Cengage Learning Australia
Level 5, 80 Dorcas Street
Southbank VIC 3006 Australia

Cengage Learning New Zealand
For learning solutions, visit **cengage.co.nz**

Printed in China by 1010 Printing International Limited.
2 3 4 5 6 7 27 26 25

walkermathsessentials

LEFT FOOT
LEFT HAND
RIGHT HAND
RIGHT FOOT
Twister
Twister

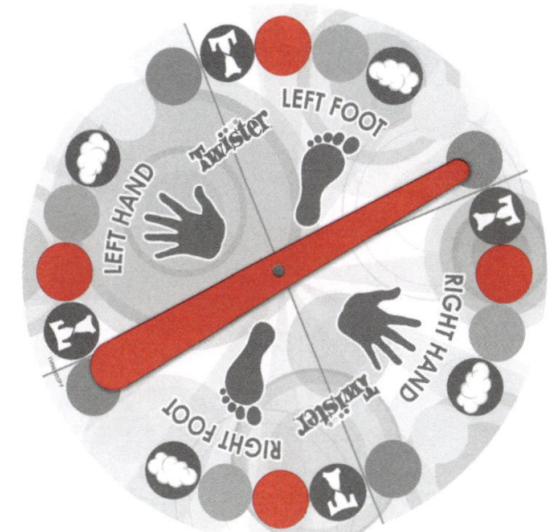

CONTENTS

Glossary

Make your own glossary of key terms:

Term	Definition	Picture/Example
Theoretical probability		
Experimental probability		
Sample space		
Outcome		
Census		
Sample		
Descriptive variable		
Discrete variable		
Continuous variable		
Proportion		
Axis (plural: axes)		
Frequency		
Mean		

ISBN: 9780170451420

Term	Definition	Picture/Example
Median		
Mode		
Range		
Unusual points		
Cluster		
Sample space		
Bias		

The statistical inquiry cycle

ISBN: 9780170451420

Probability

Fraction, decimal and percentage revision

Complete the table. Parts have been done for you.

Shaded circle picture	Fraction	Decimal	Percentage
	$\frac{3}{4}$		
		$0.\dot{6}$	
			40%
	$\frac{2}{6} = \frac{1}{3}$		$33.\dot{3}\%$

ISBN: 9780170451420

The probability scale

- A probability value tells us **how likely** it is that an event will occur.
- We use numbers between **0** and **1** to describe probability.

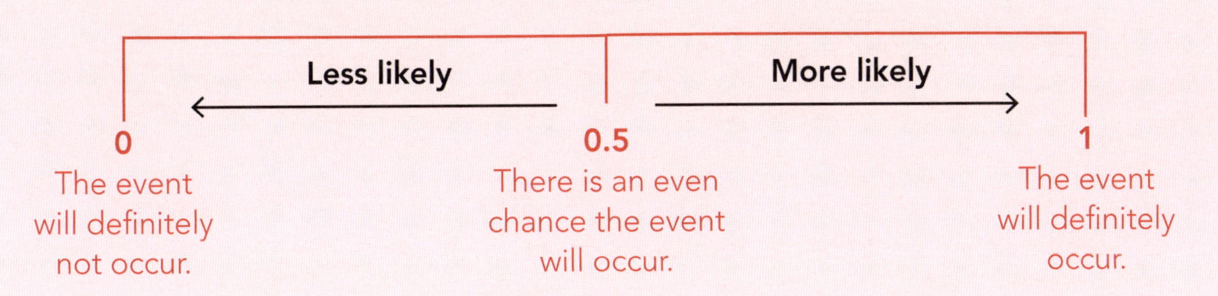

1 Discuss the meanings of these words and terms with your neighbours, and match them to their appropriate probability value. Some words may fit in several places. If you have different answers, discuss them with your teacher.

very likely	impossible	certain	slight chance	very unlikely	probable
almost certain	no way	a sure thing	definite	no chance	maybe
good chance	guaranteed	likely	even chance	unlikely	fifty-fifty

1 ______________________

0.9 ______________________

0.7 ______________________

0.5 ______________________

0.3 ______________________

0.1 ______________________

0 ______________________

ISBN: 9780170451420

Sample space

- The **sample space** is a **list of the outcomes that can occur** when we do a probability experiment.

When one event occurs, make a list.

For example:

1 If you toss a coin, there are only two outcomes: head, tail.
$\therefore$ Sample space contains two items: head, tail.

2 If you spin the spinner on the right, there are three outcomes: 1, 3, 5.

$\therefore$ Sample space contains three items: 1, 3, 5.

When two events occur, draw a probability tree or make a table.

For example: Toss a coin and then spin the spinner.

Draw a probability tree.

Use the tree to **list the outcomes** in the sample space:

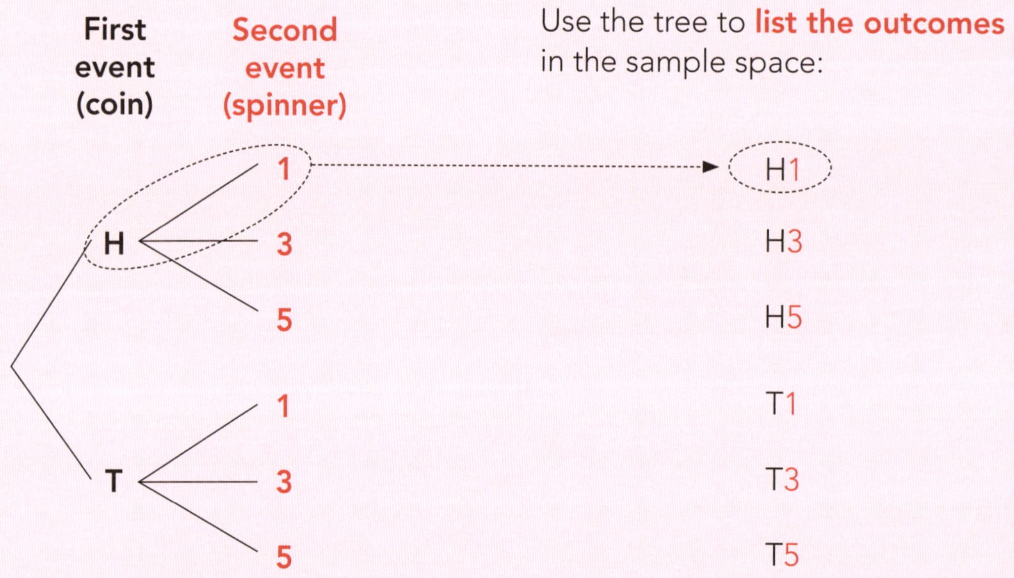

The **number of outcomes** in the sample space is 6.

Another way of calculating the number of outcomes in the sample space:

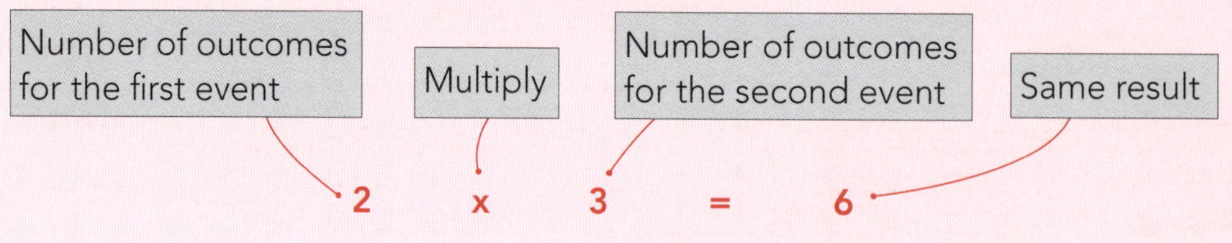

ISBN: 9780170451420

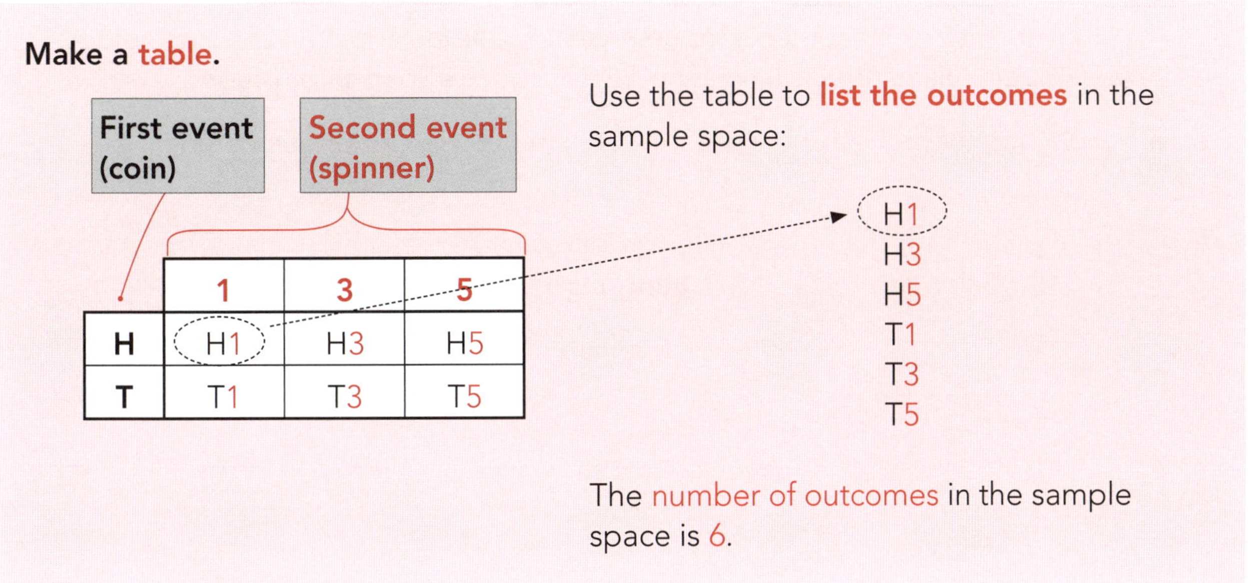

Answer the following.

1 Two coins are tossed, one after another.

a Complete the tree, list the outcomes and write the number of outcomes in the sample space.

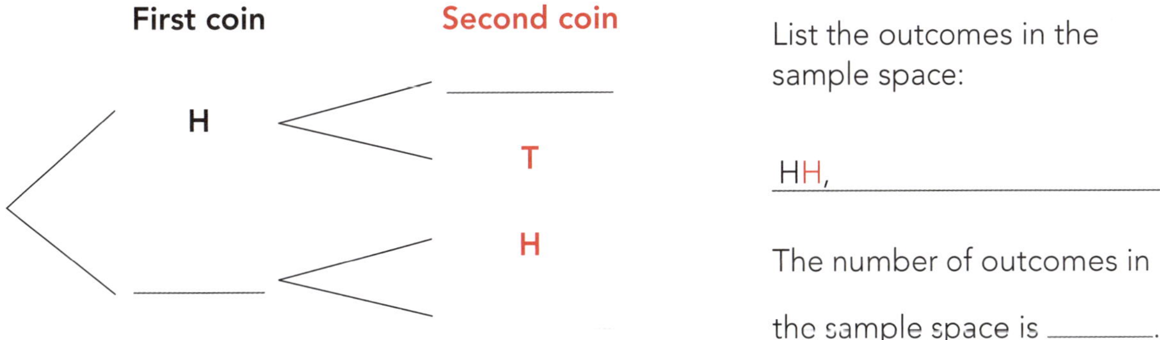

List the outcomes in the sample space:

HH, ____________________

The number of outcomes in the sample space is ______.

b Complete the table and tick if you get the same result.

	H	T
H		
T		

Same result? ☐

c Number of outcomes for the first coin = ______

Number of outcomes for the second coin = ______

Multiplying these numbers gives ______ Same result? ☐

ISBN: 9780170451420

2 Matt has to choose his subjects for next year. For science he can choose biology, physics or chemistry; for his language he can choose Spanish or Māori.

a Complete the tree and write the outcome at the end of each branch.

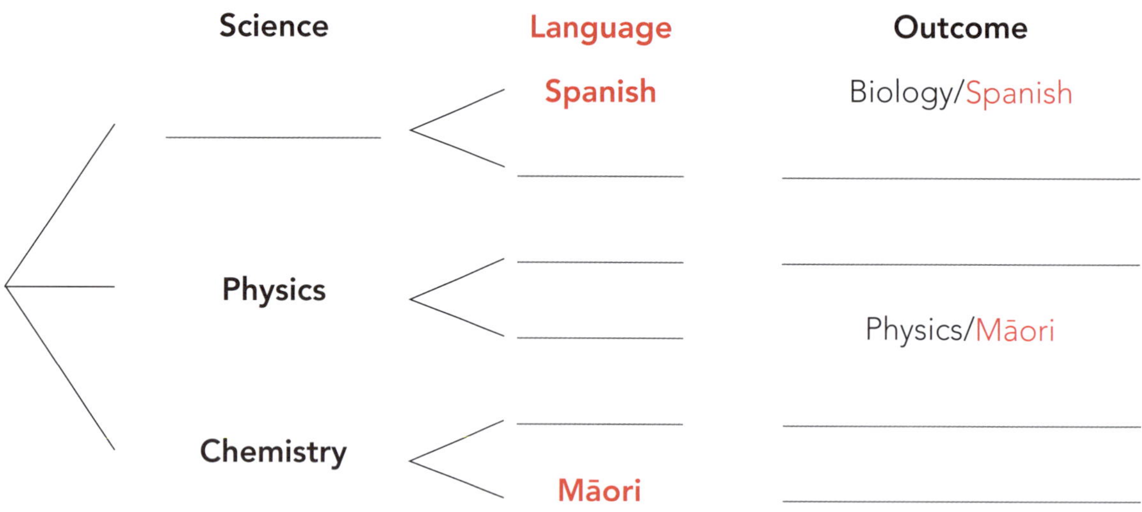

b The number of outcomes in the sample space is ________.

c Complete the table and check that you get the same result.

		Language	
		Spanish	
Science	Biology		

Same result? ☐

d number of sciences x number of languages = ______ x ______

= ______

Same result? ☐

ISBN: 9780170451420

Calculating theoretical probability

- When we use devices such as fair coins, dice and spinners, we **know** in theory the probabilities of single events.
- A **fair** coin, dice or spinner is one for which all outcomes are equally likely.
- We can use the probabilities of single events to calculate the probabilities of combined events.

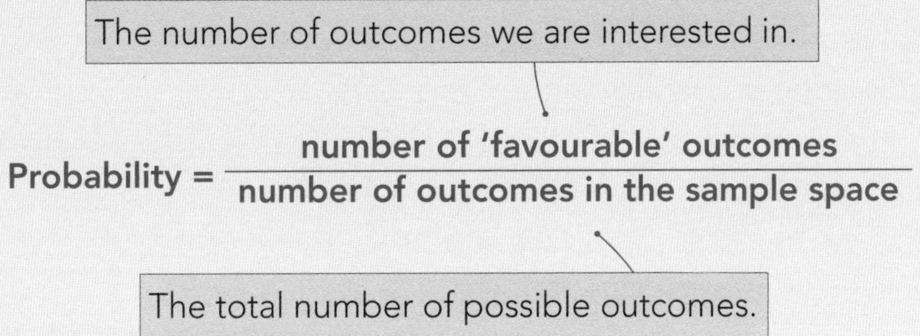

1 Where there is one event

- When there is just one event, write a **list** of all the outcomes and use it to **calculate probabilities**.
- If we want to write '**the probability of getting a 2 or a 3**', we shorten it to **P(2 or 3)**.

Example: Georgina spins the spinner.

List the outcomes (sample space): **2, 3, 4, 5, 6**

The number of outcomes in the sample space = **5**

Calculate the probability of landing on a 2, 3, 4, 5 or 6.
Every sector contains a 2, 3, 4, 5 or 6, so P(2, 3, 4, 5 or 6) = $\frac{5}{5} = 1$

Calculate the probability of landing on a 4 or a 6.
Two sectors contains a 4 or a 6, so P(4 or 6) = $\frac{2}{5}$

Calculate the probability of landing on a 7.
No sector contains a 7, so P(7) = $\frac{0}{5} = 0$

Calculate the probability of landing on a 3.
Just one sector contains a 3, so P(3) = $\frac{1}{5}$

ISBN: 9780170451420

Answer the following.

1 Keri throws a die.
Note: We talk of one **die** or more than one **dice**.

a List the possible outcomes from one throw.

____

b The number of outcomes in the sample space = ____________

c Calculate the probability of throwing a 5. P = ________

d Calculate the probability of throwing a 4 or a 6. P = ________

e Calculate the probability of throwing an odd number. P = ________

f Calculate the probability of throwing a 7. P = ________

g Calculate the probability of throwing a 1, 2, 3, 4, 5 or 6. P = ________

2 A marble is selected from the bag without looking.

a List the outcomes.

____

b The number of outcomes in the sample space = ____________

c Calculate the probability of getting a red marble. P = ________

d Calculate the probability of getting a red or white marble. P = ________

e Calculate the probability of getting a marble that isn't white. P = ________

f Calculate the probability of getting a blue marble. P = ________

g Calculate the probability of getting a marble that is either white, red or black. P = ________

ISBN: 9780170451420

2 Where there is more than one event

- When there is more than one event, probability trees and probability tables are useful ways of creating **lists** to help you **calculate probabilities**.

Example: Toss a coin and then spin the spinner. Calculate the probability of getting:

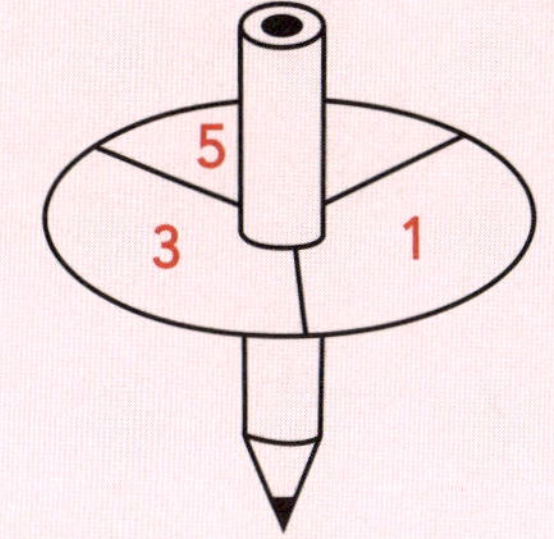

1 a head and a 3
2 a tail and a number bigger than 2.

Using a probability tree.

First event (coin)	Second event (spinner)	Outcomes
H	1	H1
H	3	H3
H	5	H5
T	1	T1
T	3	T3
T	5	T5

1 P(head and 3) $= \frac{1}{6}$

2 P(tail and number bigger than 2) $= \frac{2}{6}$ or $\frac{1}{3}$

Using a table.

1 A head and a 3.

	1	3	5
H	H1	H3	H5
T	T1	T3	T5

1 P(head and 3) $= \frac{1}{6}$

2 A tail and a number bigger than 2.

	1	3	5
H	H1	H3	H5
T	T1	T3	T5

2 P(tail and number bigger than 2) $= \frac{2}{6}$ or $\frac{1}{3}$

ISBN: 9780170451420

Answer the following.

3 Two coins are tossed, one after another.

a Use the probability tree to show how you would calculate the probability of getting two heads.

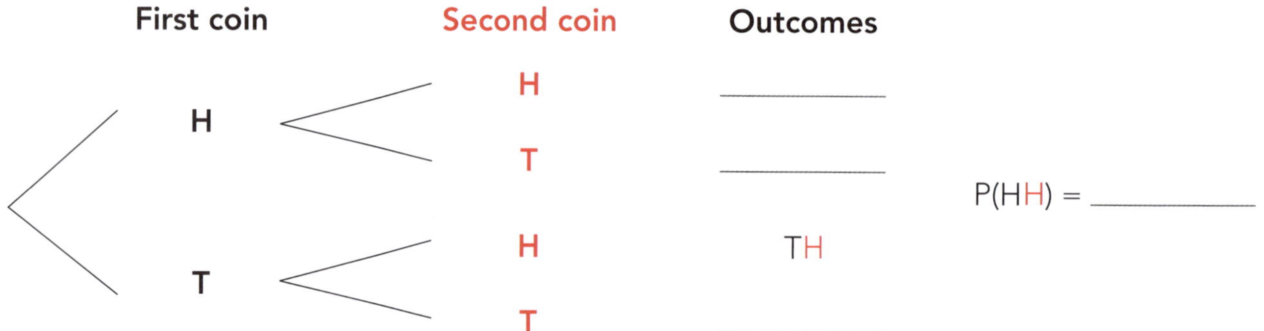

P(HH) = ____________

b Use the table to show how you would calculate the probability of getting a head and a tail in any order (TH or HT).

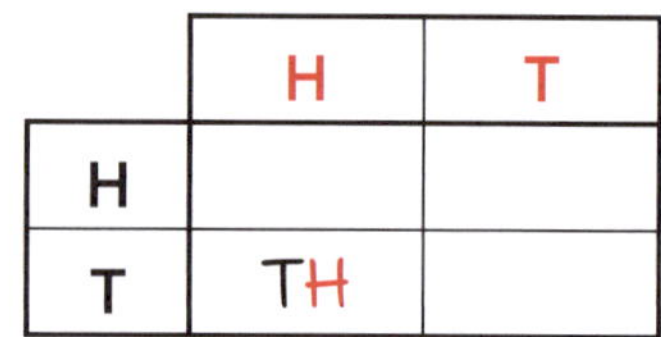

	H	T
H		
T	TH	

P(TH or HT) = ____________

c **i** Calculate the probability of getting no heads.

P(no heads) = ____________

ii Calculate the probability of getting one or two heads.

P(one or two heads) = ____________

iii What do you notice about the last two answers? Why do you think this is?

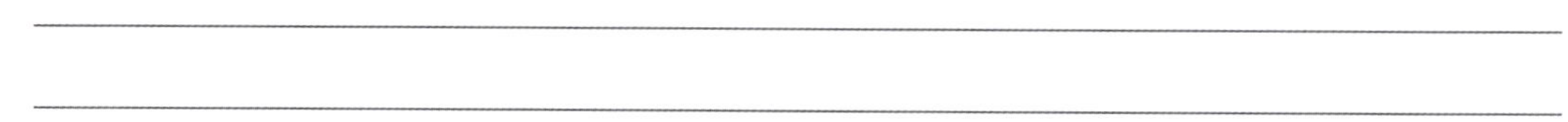

iv There are three possible outcomes for tossing two coins: two heads, two tails and one of each. Explain why each event doesn't have the same probability.

____

____

 ISBN: 9780170451420

4 A coin is tossed and then a die is thrown.

a Complete the table to show all the possible outcomes.

		Die					
				3			
Coin	H						
	T						T6

b Use the table to calculate the following probabilities.

i The probability of getting a head and a 4. P = ____________

ii The probability of getting a tail and 1 or 2. P = ____________

iii The probability of getting an even number. P = ____________

iv The probability of getting a head and an odd number. P = ____________

v The probability of getting a head and a 7. P = ____________

5 This spinner is spun and then a die is thrown, and the numbers on them are added.

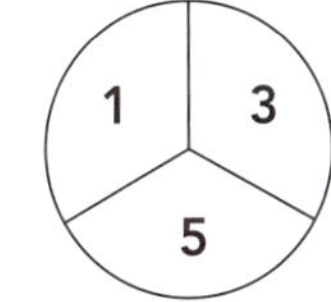

a Complete the table to show all the possible outcomes.

		Die					
		1					
Spinner							
					7		
	5						

b Use the table to calculate the following probabilities.

i The probability that the total is 11. P = ____________

ii The probability that the total is 7. P = ____________

iii The probability that the total is 12. P = ____________

iv The probability that the total is an odd number. P = ____________

ISBN: 9780170451420

Calculating probabilities based on surveys

- Sometimes it isn't possible to calculate probabilities, so we need to carry out **surveys** (or **experiments** — see next section) in order to estimate them.
E.g. the probability that the boys' tiddlywinks team will win their match on Saturday.
- In situations like this, we have to **estimate** probabilities based on **surveys**.

$$\textbf{Probability} = \frac{\textbf{number of 'favourable' outcomes}}{\textbf{number of outcomes in the sample space}}$$

Examples:

1 Here are the past results for the boys' tiddlywinks team. Based on their past performance, what is the probability that they win their next game?

Wins	6
Losses	10

There have been 16 matches so far.

There have been 6 wins.

$\therefore$ P(win next game) $= \frac{6}{16} = 0.375$

2 A survey was done of 100 shoppers in a mall. They were asked how they travelled to the mall.

Drove	Biked	Walked	Bus
53	15	11	21

P(shopper came by bus) $= \frac{21}{100} = 0.21$

P(shopper came by car or bus) $= \frac{53 + 21}{100} = 0.74$

Answer the following questions.

1 On a particular day, these were the results for cars tested at a warrant of fitness station.

Pass	25
Fail	15

a How many cars were tested? ____________

b Based on these results, what is the probability that a randomly chosen car will pass its test?

P(pass) = ____________

2 The 25 members of a class were asked which ice cream flavour they liked best: chocolate, raspberry or hokey pokey. Eight liked chocolate, seven liked raspberry and ten voted for hokey pokey.

a What is the probability that a randomly chosen class member liked hokey pokey best?

P(hokey pokey) = ____________

b What is the probability that a randomly chosen class member preferred hokey pokey or chocolate?

P(hokey pokey or chocolate) = ____________

ISBN: 9780170451420

3 Students were asked to select a language they wanted to learn.

Samoan	Te Reo	French	Japanese
15	21	13	11

a How many students were asked? __________

b What is the probability that a randomly chosen student wanted to learn Samoan? P(Samoan) = __________

c What is the probability that a randomly chosen student chose French or Japanese? P(French or Japanese) = __________

d What percentage (2 dp) did not choose Japanese? __________

4 These are the results of the hockey team so far this season.

Win	3
Draw	1
Loss	6

a How many games have they played? __________

b Based on these results, what is the probability they will win their next game?

P(win) = __________

c Based on these results, what is the probability they draw or lose their next game? P(draw or lose) = __________

5 Students went a school trip and chose to do either kayaking or orienteering.

		Activity		
		Kayaking	Orienteering	Totals
Year	Year 9	15	12	
Year	Year 10	20	13	
	Totals			

a Complete the table.

b What is the probability that a student went kayaking? P(kayaking) = __________

c What is the probability that a student was Year 10? P(Year 10) = __________

d What is the probability that a student was Year 9 and went orienteering?

P(Year 9 and orienteering) = __________

e What percentage (1 dp) of Year 10 students went kayaking? __________

ISBN: 9780170451420

Experimental probability

- Sometimes it isn't possible to calculate probabilities, so we need to carry out **experiments** (or **surveys** — see previous section) in order to estimate them.

1 Andy thinks that a coin is more likely to land on tails because there is more metal on the head side, so it should land with the heads down. Tai disagrees with him.

In order to test this, they both decide to do experiments.

Andy decides to toss a 50c coin 10 times and record the number of heads and tails.

These are his results: **H, T, T, H, H, H, T, T, T, T**.
Here is how he recorded his results:

We call the probability calculated from the results of an experiment, the **experimental probability**.

		Total	Probability	
Heads	IIII	4	$\frac{4}{10}$	0.4
Tails	~~IIII~~ I	6	$\frac{6}{10}$	0.6

Questions

a If Andy's idea was wrong, and the chance of tossing heads and tails is the same, how many tails would you expect him to get? __________

b Do you think Andy's results prove that the probability of getting a tail is greater than the probability of getting a head? Yes/No

Explain why or why not.

____

____

c What do you think Andy needs to do in order to find out if his idea is true?

____

Tai did his own experiment. He tossed a 50c coin 50 times. These were his results:

		Total	Probability	
Heads	~~IIII~~ ~~IIII~~ ~~IIII~~ ~~IIII~~ ~~IIII~~ II		$\frac{\quad}{50}$	
Tails	~~IIII~~ ~~IIII~~ ~~IIII~~ ~~IIII~~ III		$\frac{\quad}{50}$	

d Complete the table.

 ISBN: 9780170451420

e Do you think Tai's results prove that Andy's idea was wrong? Yes/No

Explain why or why not.

____

Their teacher decided that it would be good to test Andy's idea with the whole class. She organised for all 28 students to each toss a 50c coin 50 times. Their combined results are shown in this table:

	Total	Probability (4 dp)	
Heads	708	$\frac{\quad}{1400}$	
Tails	692		

f Complete the table.

g Do you think the class's results prove that Andy's idea was wrong? Yes/No

Explain why or why not.

____

h Complete the table below to show the probabilities of tossing heads and tails in each of the experiments.

Number of tosses	**10**	**50**	**1400**
P(Head)	0.4		
P(Tail)	0.6		

What happens to the probabilities as the number of tosses increases?

____

In fact, it has been shown that when you toss a coin, you are equally likely to get a head or a tail.

i How many heads would you expect to get if you tossed a coin a million times?

____

j When Andy did his experiment, he tossed a 50c coin 10 times and these were his results: **H, T, T, H, H, H, T, T, T, T**. His last four tosses produced tails.

Tai was watching him and said that if he tossed the 50c coin an eleventh time, it would probably be a head.

Do you agree with him? Yes/No

Explain why or why not.

____

Complementary events

- **Complementary** events occur when there are **only two possible outcomes**, e.g. scoring a goal or not scoring a goal.
- The probabilities of complementary events **add to 1**.

Notice this is spelt with an '**e**'. Things that are complimentary are free.

Examples:

1 When tossing a fair coin, the result must be a head or a tail.

P(head) = 0.5
P(tail) = 0.5 } 0.5 + 0.5 = 1

The events 'tossing a head' and 'tossing a tail' are complementary.

2 On a particular day, either it rains or it doesn't rain. So these events are complementary. The weather forecast says there is a 10% chance of rain.
The chance it will not rain is 100% – 10% = 90%.

3 All the students at a school answered a survey about their uniform. The options in the survey were: 'I like the uniform' or 'I don't like it'.

They found: 52% of students said they liked the uniform.
∴ P(a student didn't like the uniform) = 1 – 0.52
= 0.48

Answer the following questions.

1 On Sunday, the weather forecast says that the probability of rain is 0.3.

The probability that it won't rain = __________.

2 Ana needs to throw a 6 on a die in order to start a board game.

$P(6) = \frac{1}{6}$ P(not throwing a 6) = __________

3 Twenty-five students from another class were asked which of three crisp flavours (chicken, green onion and sea salt) they liked best:

P(student liked chicken best) = 0.36
P(student liked green onion best) = 0.20

Calculate the probability that a student liked sea salt best: P = __________

= __________

4 Nine students in a class of 25 had a pet cat in their household. Calculate the probability that a student didn't have a pet cat.

P(student didn't have a cat) = __________

= __________

ISBN: 9780170451420

Comparing probabilities

- Probabilities can be written as **fractions**, **decimals**, **percentages** or **proportions**.
- If you want to **compare** probabilities, it is usually easiest to convert them to **decimals**.
- You need to be able to convert probabilities to decimals using your calculator.

Examples: Convert these probabilities into decimals and state which is more likely.

1 $\frac{3}{4} = 0.75$ $78\% = 0.78$

More likely: 78% — 0.78 is bigger than 0.75, so 78% is more likely.

2 $\frac{5}{8} = 0.625$ $\frac{2}{3} = 0.\dot{6}$

More likely: 2 in 3 — $0.\dot{6}$ is bigger than 0.625, so 2 in 3 is more likely.

3 $\frac{2}{5} = 0.4$ $\frac{3}{8} = 0.375$

More likely: $\frac{2}{5}$

4 $\frac{4}{5} = 0.8$ $\frac{5}{6} = 0.8\dot{3}$

More likely: $\frac{5}{6}$

Convert these probabilities into decimals and state which is more likely.

1 $\frac{1}{4}$ = ________ $\frac{1}{5}$ = ________

More likely: ________

2 $\frac{4}{5}$ = ________ 79% = ________

More likely: ________

3 85% = ________ $\frac{7}{8}$ = ________

More likely: ________

4 65% = ________ $\frac{3}{5}$ = ________

More likely: ________

5 $\frac{1}{8}$ = ________ 10% = ________

More likely: ________

6 $\frac{3}{8}$ = ________ $\frac{1}{3}$ = ________

More likely: ________

7 Picking a red marble out of the bag means you win a prize. You can choose Bag A or Bag B to play with.

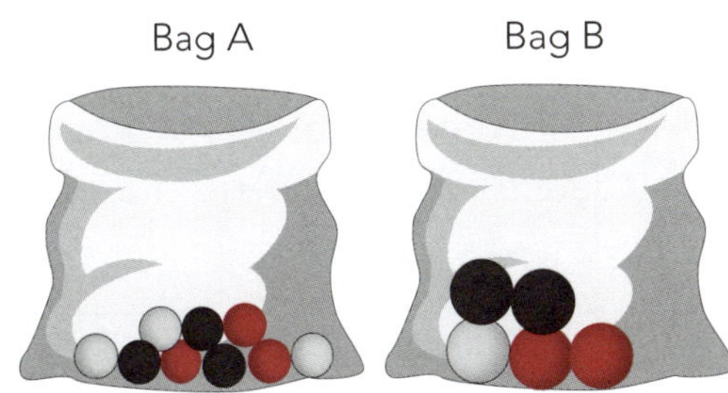

a Calculate the probability of selecting a red marble out of Bag A.

____

b Calculate the probability of selecting a red marble out of Bag B. ________

c Which bag would you choose? ________
Explain why.

____

ISBN: 9780170451420

Statistical concepts

- It's important to understand some terms and concepts that are important in Statistics.

Census and sample

A census compared with a sample

Census
- You collect data from **every member of the population**.
- You get very accurate information.
- However, it is often impossible and usually very expensive to do.
- It is best to do a census if the answer to the question **really matters**.
- In New Zealand, a census of the population takes place every five years.

Sample
- You collect data from **just some of the population**.
- The information you get will not be as accurate.
- However, it is much easier and cheaper to take a sample.
- It's important that the sample is selected ***fairly***.

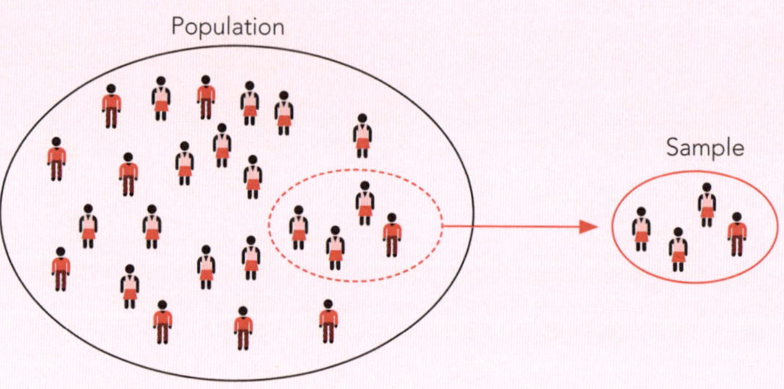

Which would be more appropriate to answer these questions and why?

	Question	Census or sample?	Why?
1	What is the North Island's favourite radio station?		
2	How many workers at a small factory own an Android phone?		
3	What is the favourite subject of New Zealand high school students?		
4	Should New Zealand change its form of government?		

ISBN: 9780170451420

Types of variables

There are three type of variables:

Descriptive variables These are descriptions or names.
Data recorded about each person/thing: **words**.
Typical question starts with 'What …'
Examples: colour, type of pet, favourite something.

Discrete variables These are **numbers** which are the result of **counting**.
Data recorded about each person/thing: **whole numbers**.
Typical question starts with 'How many …'
Examples: number of pets, number of T-shirts.

Continuous variables These **numbers** are the result of **measuring**.
They can be **fractions** or **decimals**.
Typical question starts with 'How long, heavy, etc. …'
Examples: height, weight, distance, time.

Highlight the correct variable type for each of these.

1	Ice cream flavour	Descriptive	Discrete	Continuous
2	Hand length	Descriptive	Discrete	Continuous
3	Number of siblings	Descriptive	Discrete	Continuous
4	Height	Descriptive	Discrete	Continuous

Here is some data:

Question		**Joanna**	**Max**	**Mitchell**	**Josie**
A	How many pets do you have?	3	2	0	4
B	How long is your index finger?	79 mm	82 mm	63 mm	71 mm
C	What is your favourite chocolate bar?	Crunchie	Bounty	Moro	Cherry Ripe
D	How do you get to school?	Bus	Car	Walk	Bike
E	How many texts have you had today?	17	52	3	41
F	How heavy is your school bag?	5.2 kg	3.8 kg	4.1 kg	6.3 kg

5 Which questions have answers that are descriptive variables? ______________

6 Which questions have answers that are discrete variables? ______________

7 Which questions have answers that are continuous variables? ______________

ISBN: 9780170451420

Investigative questions

- There are **three** types of investigative questions:

Summary questions: investigate **one variable** at a time. This could be a word or a number.

Examples: What is your favourite fruit? — **One variable** — fruit.
How many pets do you have? — **One variable** — number of pets.

Comparative questions: investigate **one variable** for **two groups**.

Example: Did the boys get higher grades than the girls in the science test?

One variable — science grade. **Two groups** — girls and boys.

Relationship questions: compare **two variables** for **one group**.

Example: Is there a relationship between height and arm span in Year 9 students?

Two variables — height and arm span. **One group** — Year 9 students.

Highlight which type of question these are.

	Question	Type of question
1	What colour is your hair?	Summary Comparative Relationship
2	Do Year 9 students sleep for longer than Year 10 students?	Summary Comparative Relationship
3	Is it quicker to bike home or skateboard?	Summary Comparative Relationship
4	What is your favourite ice cream flavour?	Summary Comparative Relationship
5	Is there a relationship between the age of a house and its sale price?	Summary Comparative Relationship
6	How many pens did you bring to school?	Summary Comparative Relationship
7	Does the age of students at Paradise High School influence the time spent doing homework?	Summary Comparative Relationship
8	Do electric cars accelerate faster than petrol cars?	Summary Comparative Relationship

ISBN: 9780170451420

Data display

- There are different ways of displaying data. Which is most appropriate depends on the **type** of variable:

Descriptive data	Discrete data	Continuous data
Tally chart Pictograph Strip graph Pie graph Dot plot Bar graph	Tally chart Pictograph Strip graph Line graph Dot plot Bar graph	Histogram Line graph/time series Scatter plot

Match these types of graph to the images below.

Pie chart	Histogram	Tally chart
Bar graph	Dot plot	Strip graph
Line graph/time series	Pictograph	Scatter plot

1

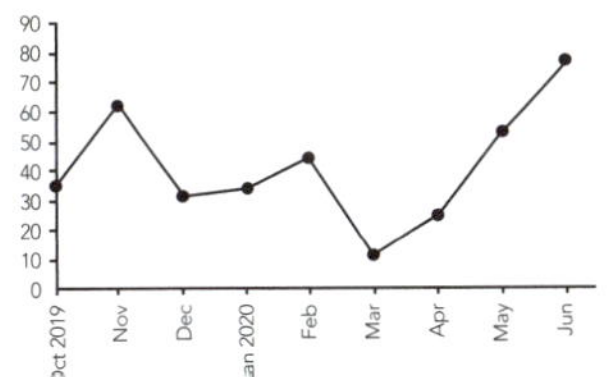

____

2

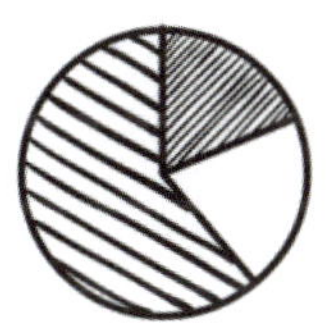

____

3

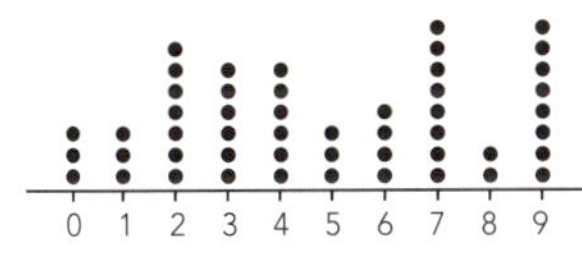

____

4

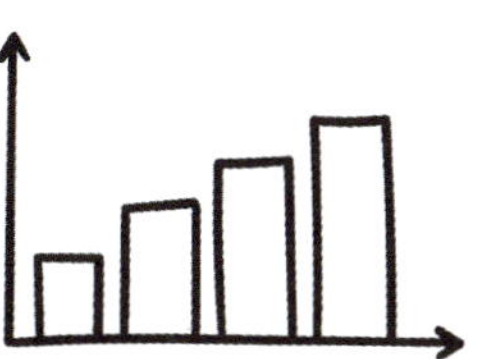

____

5

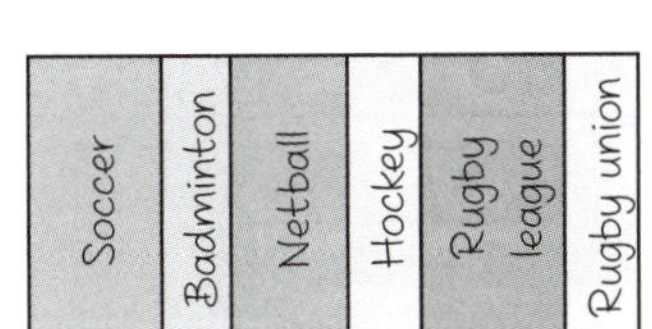

____

6

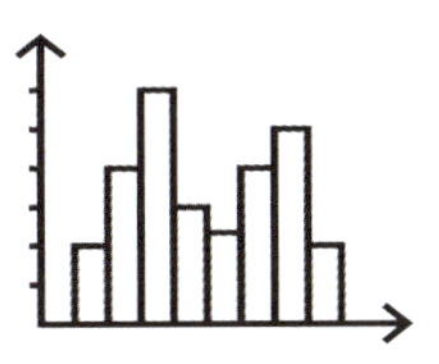

____

7

French	||||
German	~~||||~~ ||||
Latin	||
Spanish	~~||||~~

____

8

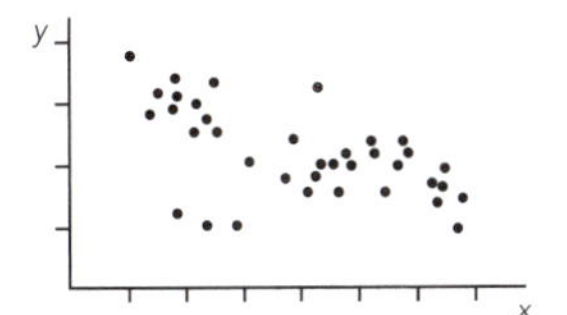

____

9

____

All sorts of other graphs are used, but remember, fancy doesn't necessarily mean better or easier to understand.

ISBN: 9780170451420

Tally charts and frequency tables

- Tally charts are used when you are counting **descriptive** or **discrete** variables.
- You add the tallies to get the frequencies.

Understanding tally charts and frequency tables

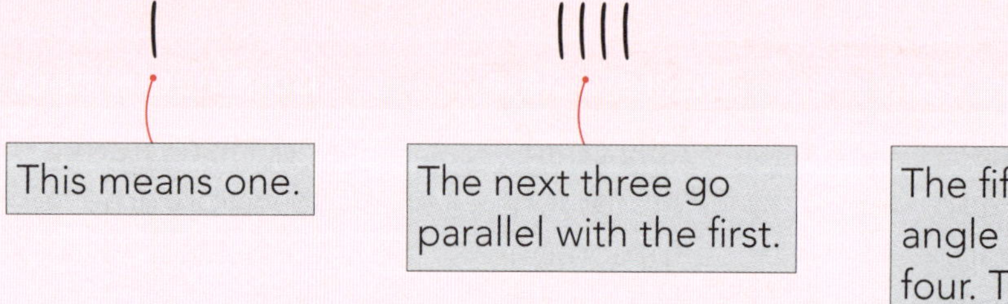

The fifth is drawn on an angle across the other four. Then it is easy to add up the sets of 5.

Example: All the members of a class were asked 'What is your favourite type of fruit?' The results are shown in this table.

The tallies are added and the total is written in the frequency column.

Favourite fruit	Tally	Frequency
Kiwifruit	𝍸 ||	7
Apple	𝍸 |	6
Watermelon	||||	4
Banana	|||	3
Strawberry	𝍸 𝍸	10
	Total	**30**

1 How many students were in the class? 7 + 6 + 4 + 3 + 10 = 30 students

2 How many students said their favourite was strawberries or melon? 10 + 4 = 14

3 What is the probability that a student said their favourite was apples? $P = \frac{6}{30} = 0.2$

4 Highlight the type of question that was asked: Summary Comparative Relationship

 ISBN: 9780170451420

Answer the following questions.

1 The table shows the numbers of main courses ordered in a restaurant during one hour.

Dinner choice	**Tally**	**Frequency**
Spaghetti	𝍸 I	
Pizza	𝍸 𝍸 II	
Burrito	IIII	
Steak	𝍸 III	
	Total	

a Complete the table.

b How many main courses were ordered? __________

c What was the most popular order? __________

d What is the probability that somebody ordered spaghetti? __________

2 Members of a class of 25 students were asked to pick their favourite emoticon.

Favourite emoticon	**Tally**	**Frequency**
😝	𝍸 𝍸 I	
😊		0
😍	𝍸 II	
😮		5
😠		2
	Total	

a Complete the missing tallies and frequencies.

b What was the most popular emoticon? __________

c What is the probability that a student liked 😠 best? __________

Creating tally charts and frequency tables

Example: Students were asked which of these things they would like for their birthday.

Here are the results:

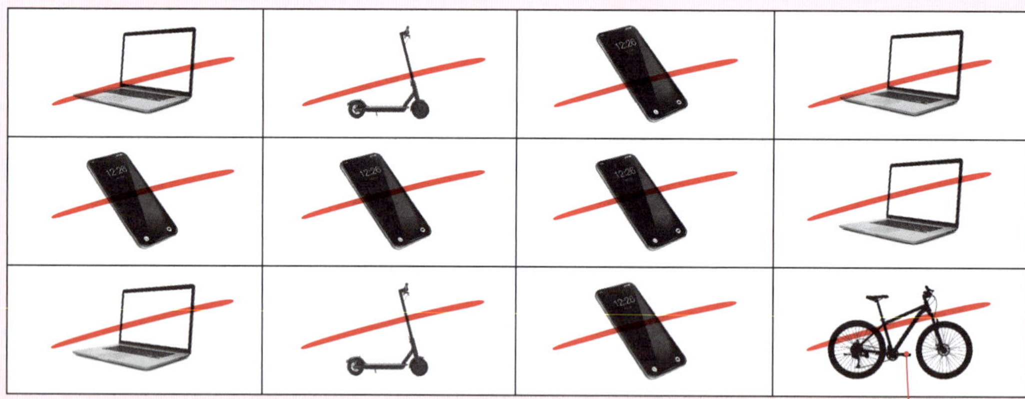

<table>
<tr><th>Item</th><th>Tally</th><th>Frequency</th></tr>
<tr><td></td><td>𝍸</td><td>5</td></tr>
<tr><td></td><td>|</td><td>1</td></tr>
<tr><td></td><td>||</td><td>2</td></tr>
<tr><td></td><td>||||</td><td>4</td></tr>
<tr><td></td><td>Total</td><td>12</td></tr>
</table>

Cross out each object when you add its tally stroke.

Adding the total is sensible.

3 **a** What was the least popular birthday present? ______________

b How many students wanted something electronic? ______________

c What is the probability that a student wanted something with two wheels? ______________

 ISBN: 9780170451420

4 Jemma and her friends wrote down what sort of pet they would like. These are her results.

a Complete the tally chart.

Item	Tally	Frequency
	|	
	|	
	Total	

b What was the most popular pet? ________________

c How many friends did she ask? ________________

d What is the probability that a friend wanted a cat? ________________

ISBN: 9780170451420

Pictographs

- Pictographs use pictures to show **descriptive** and **discrete** data.
- Assume each picture represents one person or thing unless you are told otherwise.

Understanding pictographs

Examples:

1 Students had a choice of sport they could play. These are the results. Each symbol represents the choice of one person.

Sport	
Soccer	⚽ ⚽ ⚽
Hockey	🏑 🏑 🏑 🏑 🏑
Netball	🏐 🏐 🏐 🏐
Badminton	🏸 🏸

a What was the most popular sport? Hockey

b Which sport had only two students wanting to play it? Badminton

c How many students were asked? 14

2 This pictograph displays how many awards each student has received. 🏆 = 2 awards

Name	Number of awards
Caleb	🏆
Manawai	🏆 🏆 🏆
Trae	🏆 🏆 🏆 ½🏆
Elouise	🏆 🏆 ½🏆
Hemi	½🏆

a Who got the most awards? Trae

b How many did he get? 7

c What fraction of the awards were won by Caleb? $\frac{2}{21}$

  ISBN: 9780170451420

Answer the following questions.

1 Students were asked 'What would you like to eat at the end-of-year class lunch?' The results are shown in the table. Each symbol represents the choice of one student.

Food	
Hamburger	
Pizza	
Salad	
Hotdog	
Sushi	

a How many students were in the class? ____________

b How many students wanted a hamburger or a pizza? ____________

c What is the probability that a student didn't want pizza? ____________

2 This table shows the number of ice creams sold over four days. One ice cream symbol represents six ice creams ( = 6 ice creams).

Days of the week	
Friday	
Saturday	
Sunday	
Monday	

a On what day were exactly 15 ice creams sold? ____________

b How many ice creams altogether were sold over the four days? ____________

c What fraction of the ice creams were sold on Sunday? ____________

ISBN: 9780170451420

Creating pictographs

- When creating pictographs, use pictures that are simple to draw and easy to copy.
- Pictures should be similar sizes and lined up in columns.

Example: Jeremiah noted the weather each day for two weeks.

~~Sunny~~	~~Raining~~	~~Partly cloudy~~	~~Cloudy~~	~~Raining~~	~~Cloudy~~	~~Sunny~~
~~Raining~~	~~Sunny~~	~~Raining~~	~~Sunny~~	~~Cloudy~~	~~Partly cloudy~~	~~Raining~~

Weather	
Sunny	☼ ☼ ☼ ☼
Cloudy	☁ ☁ ☁
Partly cloudy	⛅ ⛅
Raining	🌧 🌧 🌧 🌧 🌧

Cross out each word when you add its symbol.

3 Jules surveyed her class about their feelings towards mathematics. Put the results into a pictogram. The first three have been done for you.

~~Dislike it~~	~~Love it~~	~~It's okay~~	It's okay	It's okay
Love it	It's okay	Dislike it	It's okay	Love it
It's okay	Dislike it	It's okay	Love it	Love it
Dislike it	Dislike it	Love it	It's okay	It's okay

Feeling	
Love it	☺
It's okay	😐
Dislike it	☹

Answer the following questions.

a What type of data is this? Descriptive Discrete Continuous

b How many students either love mathematics or think it's okay? __________

c What is the probability a member of the class dislikes mathematics? __________

 ISBN: 9780170451420

Pie graphs

- Pie graphs are appropriate for **descriptive** data.
- They are best used when there are relatively few divisions of the data.
- The area of each sector is proportional to the frequency of each variable. This means the biggest group has the biggest sector.

Understanding pie graphs

Examples:

1 A group of Christchurch people were asked where they would like to go for the weekend. Here are the results:

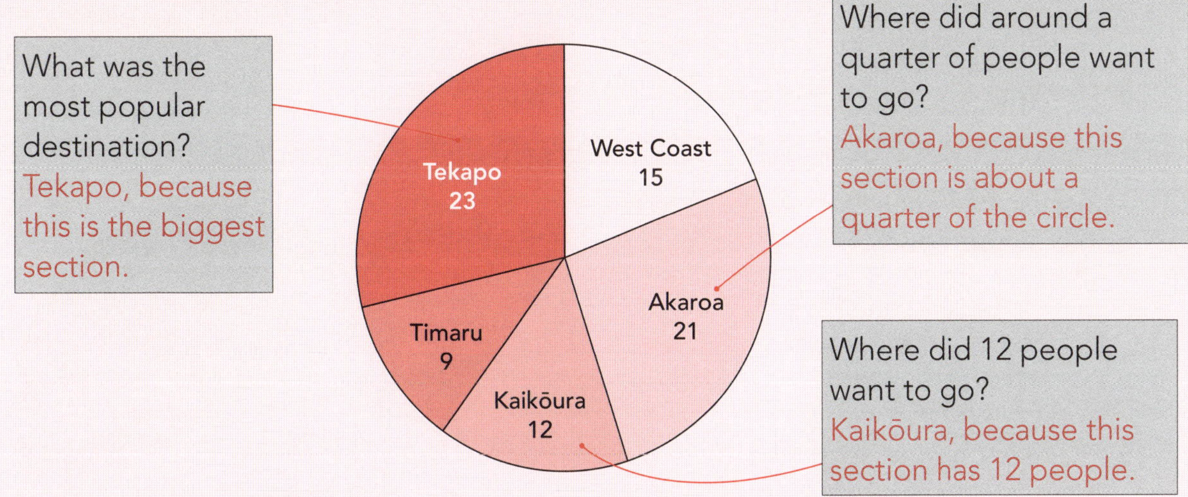

2 72 students were surveyed about their preferred lunchtime location.
In this case, numbers aren't included in the sectors so a calculation is required.

Step 1: Count how many sections there are. There are 24 sections.

Step 2: Divide the number surveyed by the number of sections: $\frac{72}{24} = 3$
∴ Each section represents **3** students.

Number of students (72); Number of sections (24)

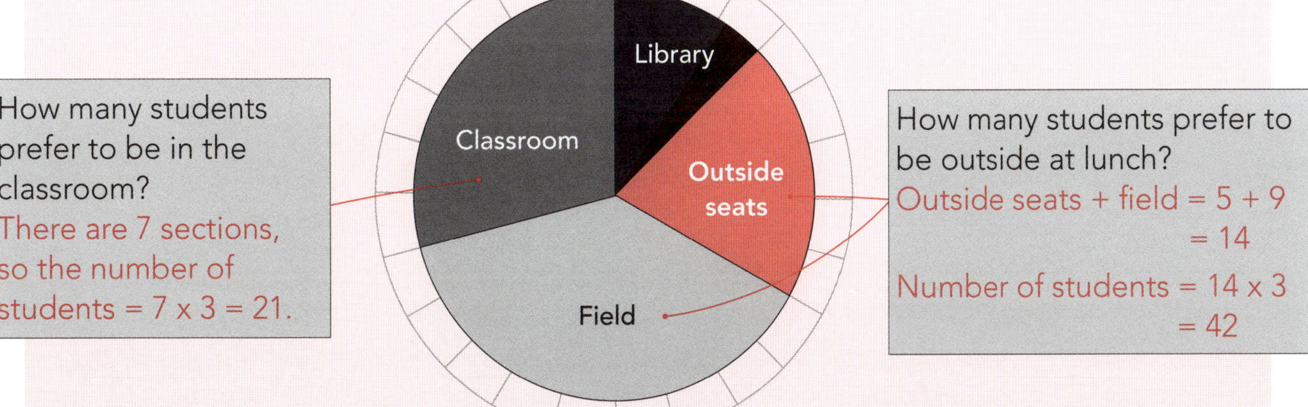

ISBN: 9780170451420

Answer the following questions.

1 Anahera surveyed the colours of cars in the mall carpark.

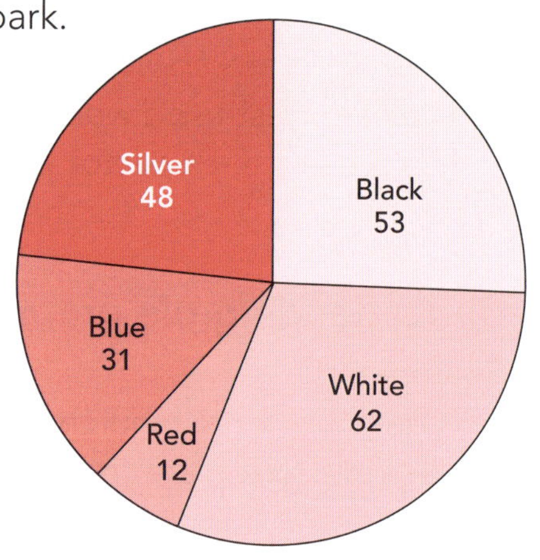

a What was the most common colour?

b Of the colours on the pie chart, what was the least common colour?

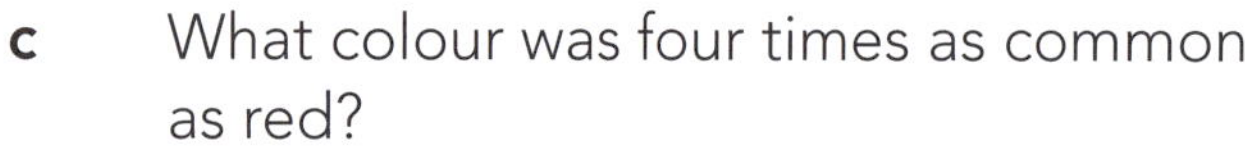

c What colour was four times as common as red?

d What fraction of the cars were red or blue?

2 Jared asked 80 students about how they got to school today.

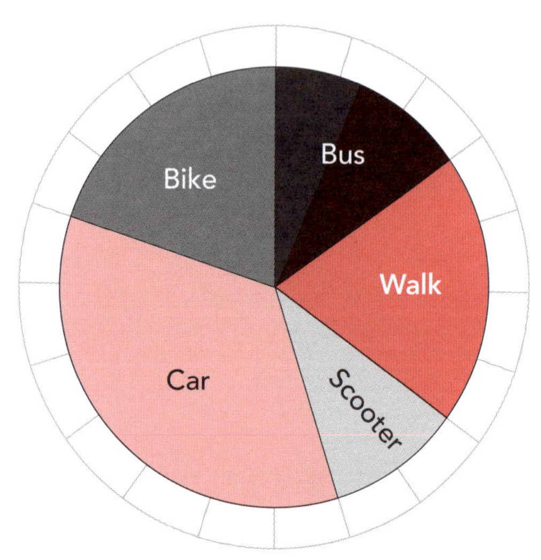

a How many students are represented by each section?

b How many students scootered to school?

c How many came by bus or car?

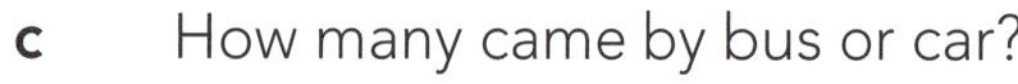

d What is the probability that a student walked or scootered to school?

3 August recorded the hair colour of 40 students. Angles in this diagram are 180°, 90° or 45°.

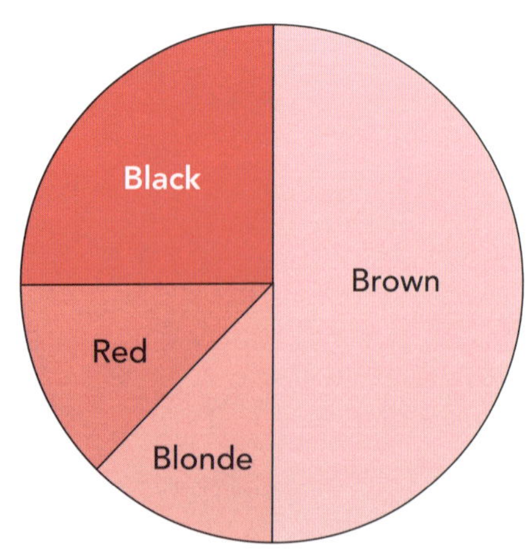

a How many students had brown hair?

b How many student had either black or blonde hair?

c Calculate the probability that a student had red or brown hair.

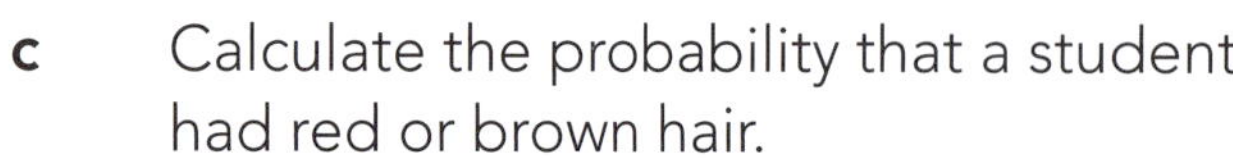

d What is the probability that a student was not blonde?

ISBN: 9780170451420

Creating pie graphs

Example: Some students were asked which type of movie they preferred. Put the results into this pie graph.

Type	Frequency
Horror	12
Romance	4
Action	8
Drama	4
Sci-fi	4
Total	**32**

Find the total.

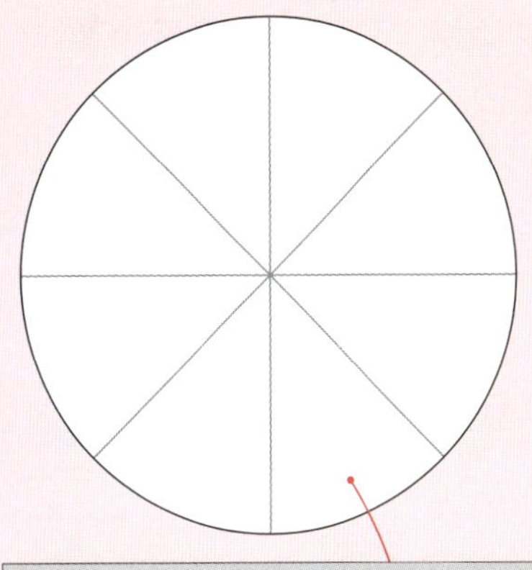

The circle has been divided into 8 equal sectors.

Each sector will represent $\dfrac{\text{number of students}}{\text{number of sectors}} = \dfrac{32}{8} = 4$ students.

To work out how many sectors make up each category, divide the frequency by 4.

Type	Frequency	Sectors
Horror	12	3
Romance	4	1
Action	8	2
Drama	4	1
Sci-fi	4	1

Sectors in Horror $= \dfrac{12}{4} = 3$

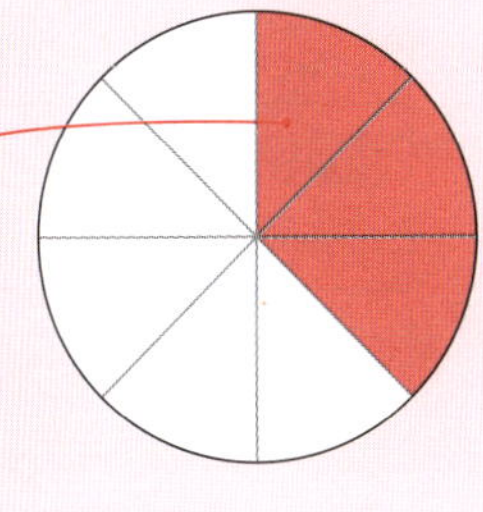

Complete the rest of the pie graph:

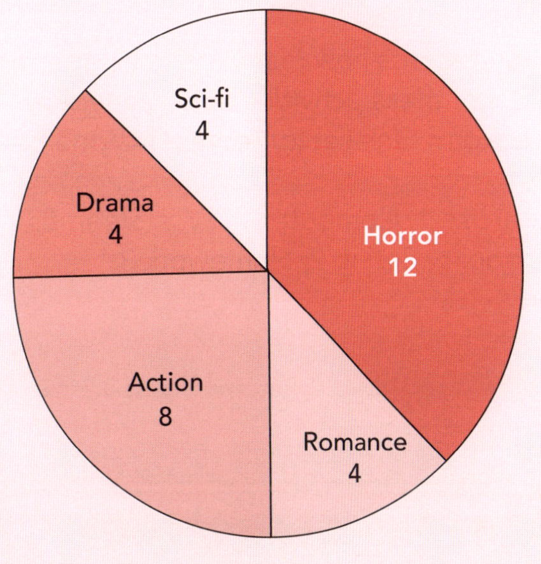

ISBN: 9780170451420

Create pie graphs for these data sets.

4 Kristen recorded how her classmates travelled to school.

Type	Frequency	Sectors
Walk	9	
Bike	3	
Car	3	
Bus	6	
Scooter	3	
Total		

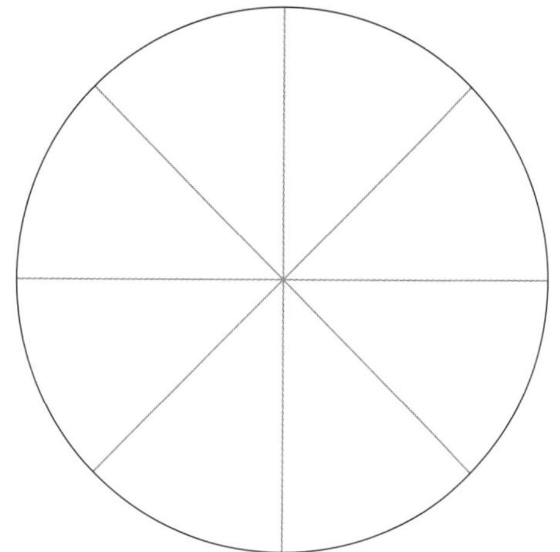

5 Jai surveyed people to find their favourite flavour of potato chips.

Type	Frequency	Sectors
Salt and vinegar	15	
Ready salted	3	
Chicken	12	
Sour cream and chives	3	
Other		
Total	**36**	

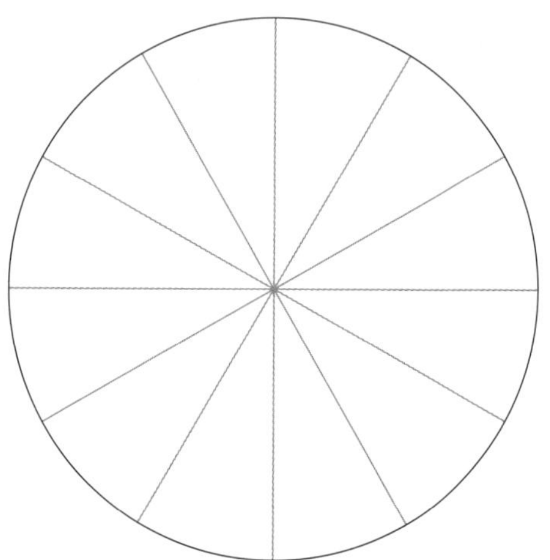

6 Juan records how many hours he spends on each of these activities during a typical weekday. One sector represents one hour.

Exercise 1, Computer 1, TV 3, Sleep 8, School 6, Eating 2, Homework 3

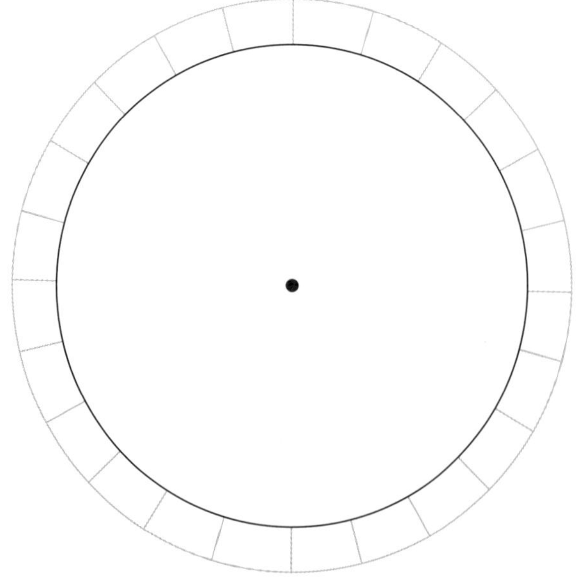

 ISBN: 9780170451420

Strip graphs

- Strip graphs can be used with **descriptive** or **discrete** numeric variables.
- They take the form of a rectangular strip which is divided into parts that are different colours or shades.
- The **length** of each part is **proportional to the frequency** of each variable.
- Sometimes they are divided into equal sections, with each section representing the same number of pieces of data.

Understanding strip graphs

Examples:

1 A group of people were asked about their eye colour. Each section represents one person. These are the results:

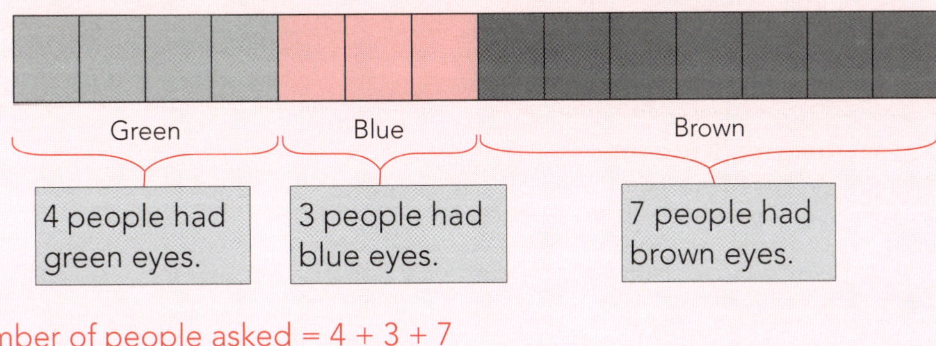

Number of people asked = 4 + 3 + 7
= 14

2 This is how Jo spent her birthday money. Each section represents $10.

a How much money did she spend on sunglasses?

Amount = 5 x $10
= $50

b How much money did she spend in total?

Amount = 13 x $10
= $130

3 For two hours Jo kept a record of the numbers of each species of bird coming to her bird feeder.

a One species tended to be bullies. Which do you think it was and why?

Tūī, because they fed the most.

b Which species made exactly double the number of visits to the feeder compared with another species? Use a ruler to check your answer.

Sparrows

ISBN: 9780170451420

1 The class was asked to write down the number of pens they brought to school today. Each square represents two students.

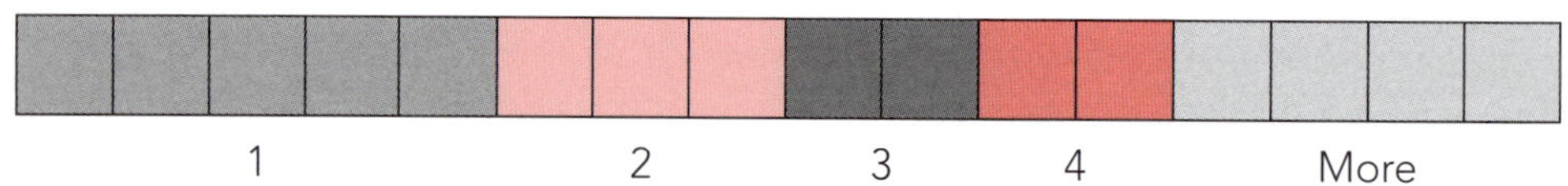

a How many had one or two pens? ____________

b How many had at least four pens? ____________

c What is the probability that a student brought only two pens to school? ____________

2 Students were asked to list the pets they have at home. Each section represents 5 animals.

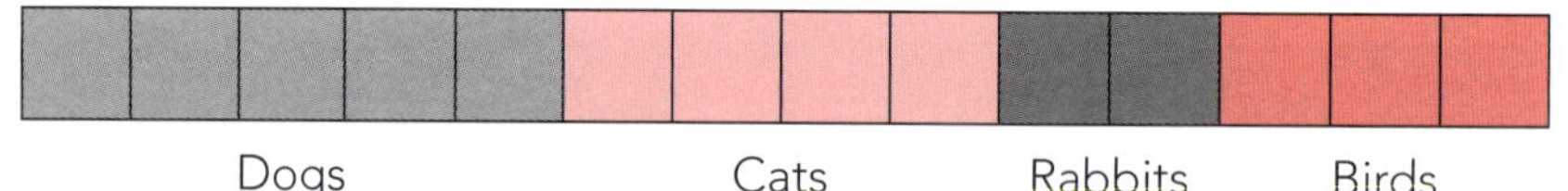

a How many cats are there? ____________

b How many pets are there in total? ____________

c What is the probability that a pet was either a rabbit or a bird? ____________

3 Three students kept track of how much they earnt at their holiday jobs.

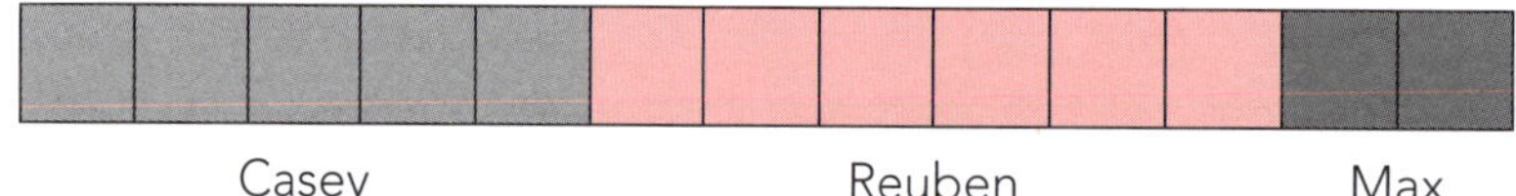

a Who earnt the most? ____________

b In total they earnt $650. How much money does each section represent? ____________

c How much did Casey earn? ____________

4 The masses of items in Trudy's tramping pack are shown in this graph:

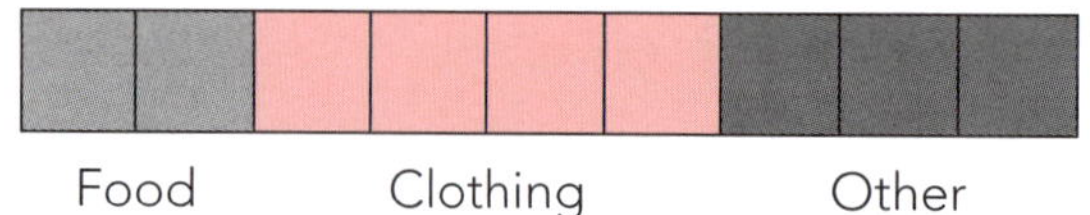

a Her pack mass is 18 kg. How much is each section worth? ____________

b What mass is her clothing? ____________

c Complete the sentence: Her ________________ weighed twice as much as her ________________.

ISBN: 9780170451420

Creating strip graphs

Example: Students were asked 'What colour is your sun hat?' These were their responses:

Red, Black, White, Black, Black, Grey, Black, White, White, Grey

First count the number of people asked.

With a total of 10 students, you will need 10 even boxes:

Count how many of each colour you will need: Red =1, Black = 4, White = 3, Grey = 2. Colour or shade the boxes appropriately.

Red	Black				White			Grey	

Draw strip graphs for the following data.

5 The student council is made up of student volunteers from different year levels.

Year 13: 3 Year 12: 4 Year 11: 2 Year 10: 1 Year 9: 3

6 Students were asked what their favourite school subject was. Put the information on a strip graph.

PE, Maths, PE, Science, Music, Art, Maths, English, Maths, Science, Science, Maths, English, PE, PE, Science

ISBN: 9780170451420

Reading axes

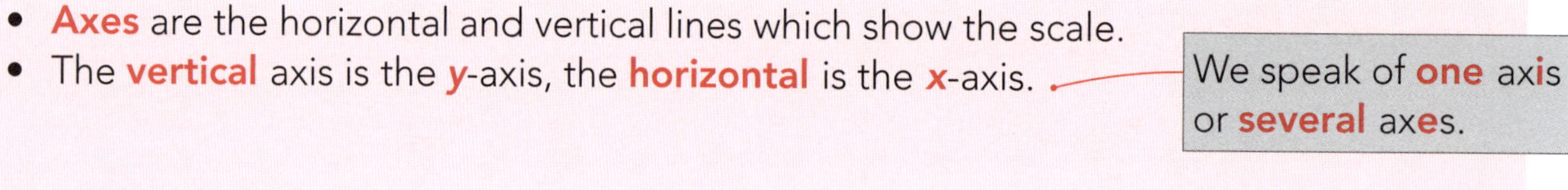

- **Axes** are the horizontal and vertical lines which show the scale.
- The **vertical** axis is the *y*-axis, the **horizontal** is the *x*-axis.

We speak of **one** axis or **several** axes.

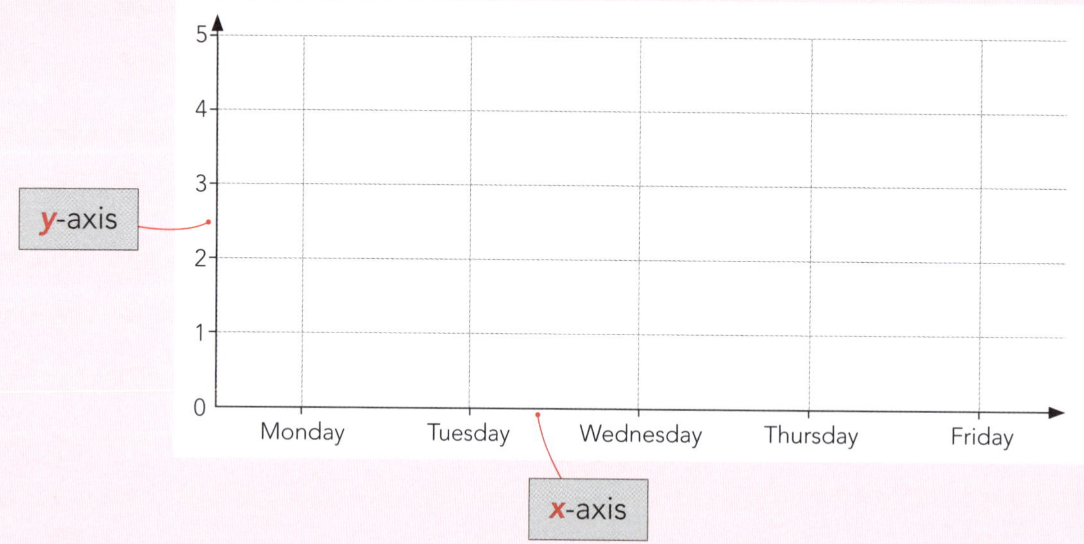

Examples:

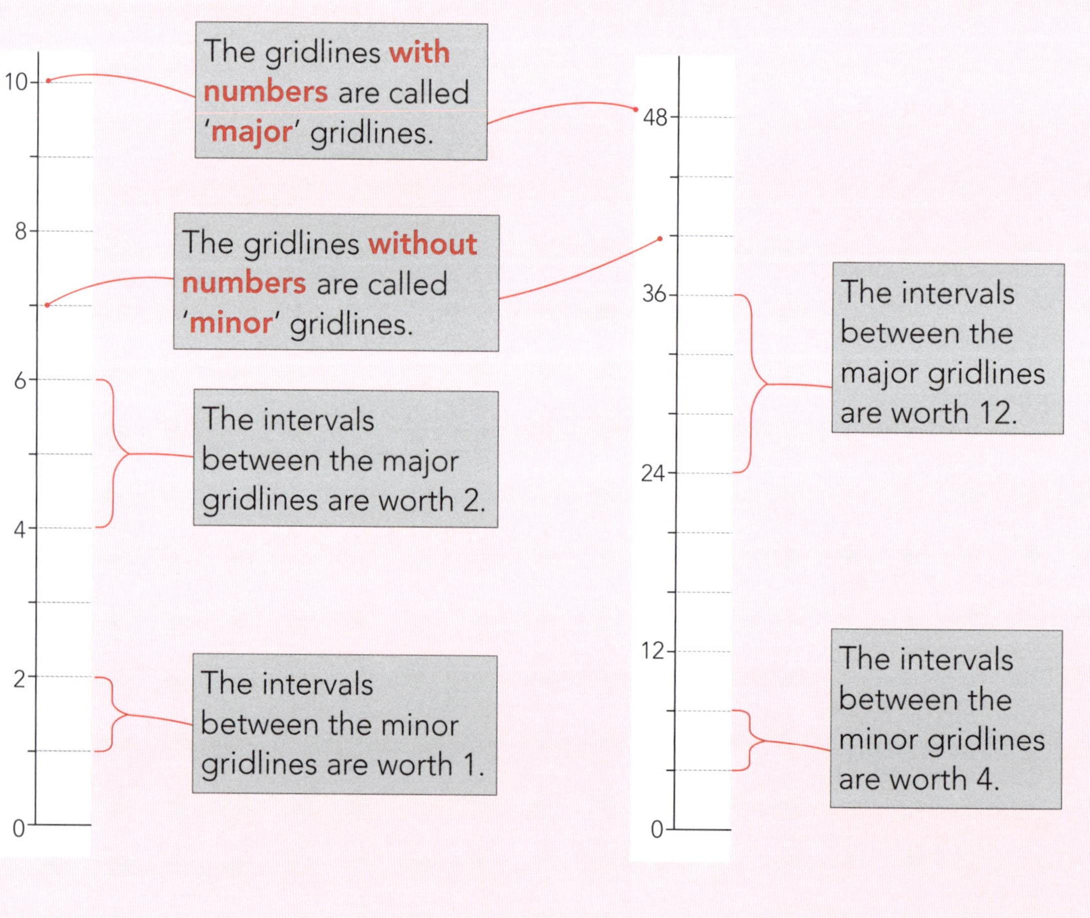

 ISBN: 9780170451420

Write down the major and minor intervals, and then fill in the missing values on these axes.

1 Major ________ Minor ________

2 Major ________ Minor ________

3 Major ________ Minor ________

4 Major ________ Minor ________

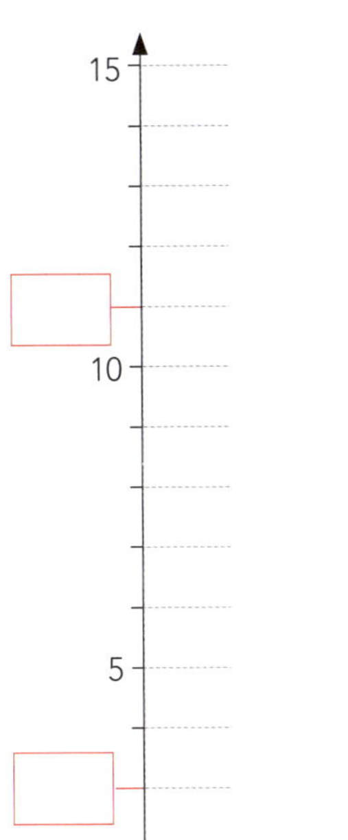

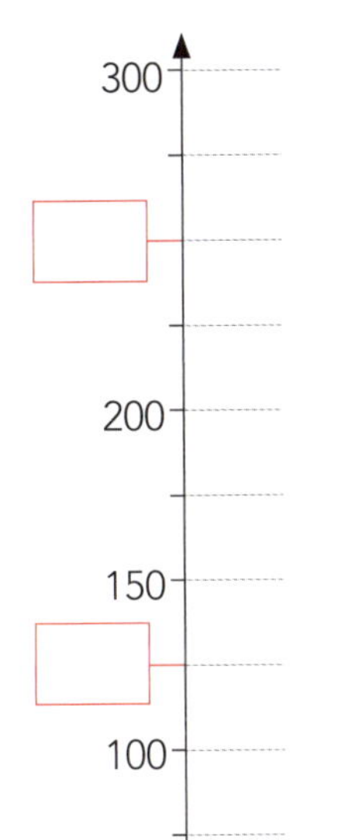

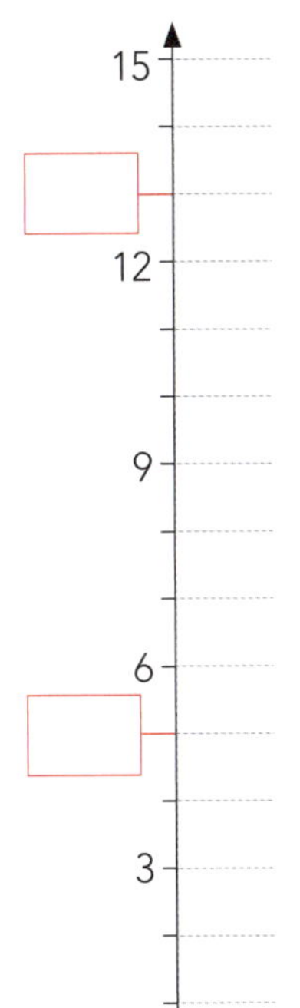

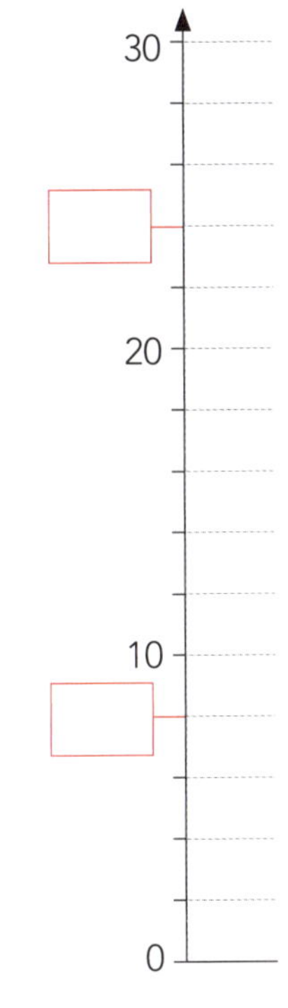

5 Major ________ Minor ________

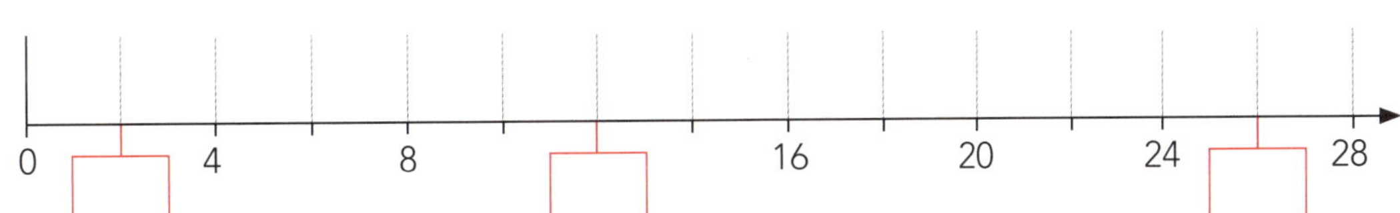

6 Major ________ Minor ________

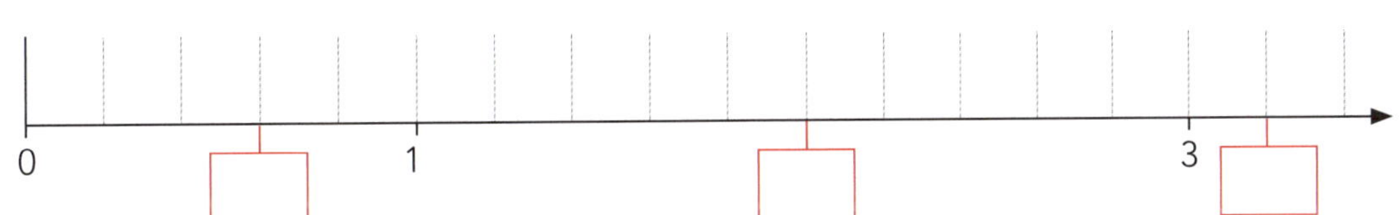

Bar graphs

- Bar graphs are used to display **discrete** or **descriptive** data.
- They are sometimes known as column graphs.
- They can be plotted **vertically** or **horizontally**.
- The bars always have **gaps** between them.

Understanding bar graphs

Examples:

1 Data were collected on the months in which students in 9A had birthdays.

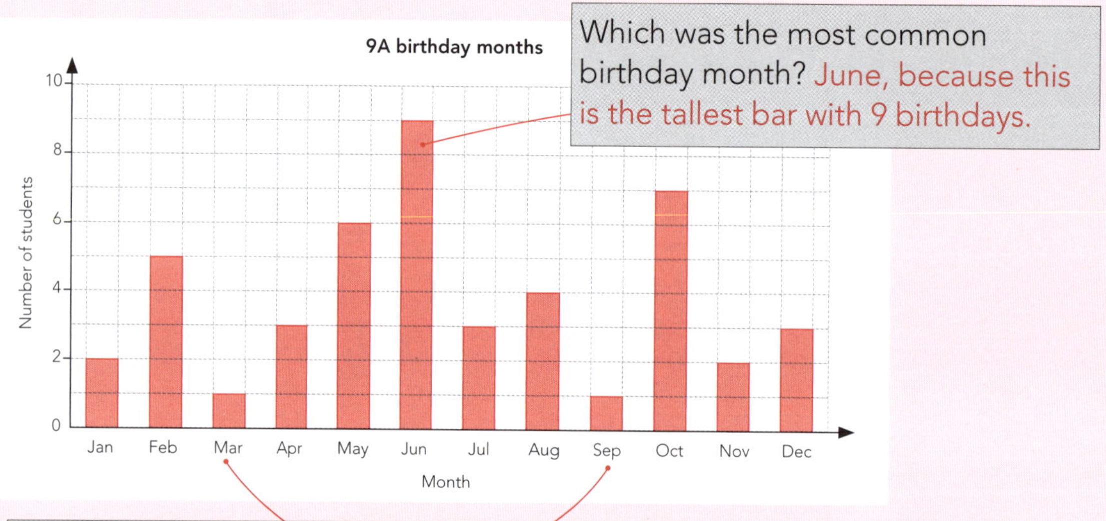

Which were the least common birthday months? March and September, because they have the shortest bars, with 1 birthday in each.

2 **Several groups** can be plotted on the same graph. Birthday months were also collected for students in 9B and 9C.

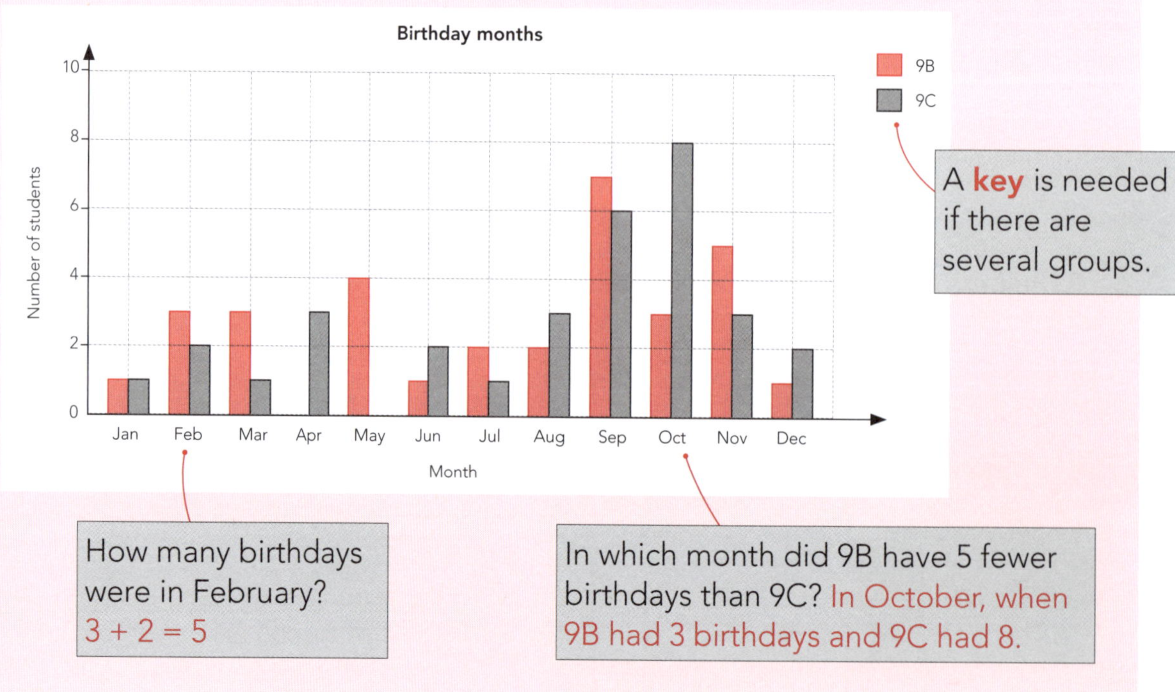

ISBN: 9780170451420

3 Bar graphs can also be displayed **horizontally**. Data were collected on students' favourite ice cream flavours.

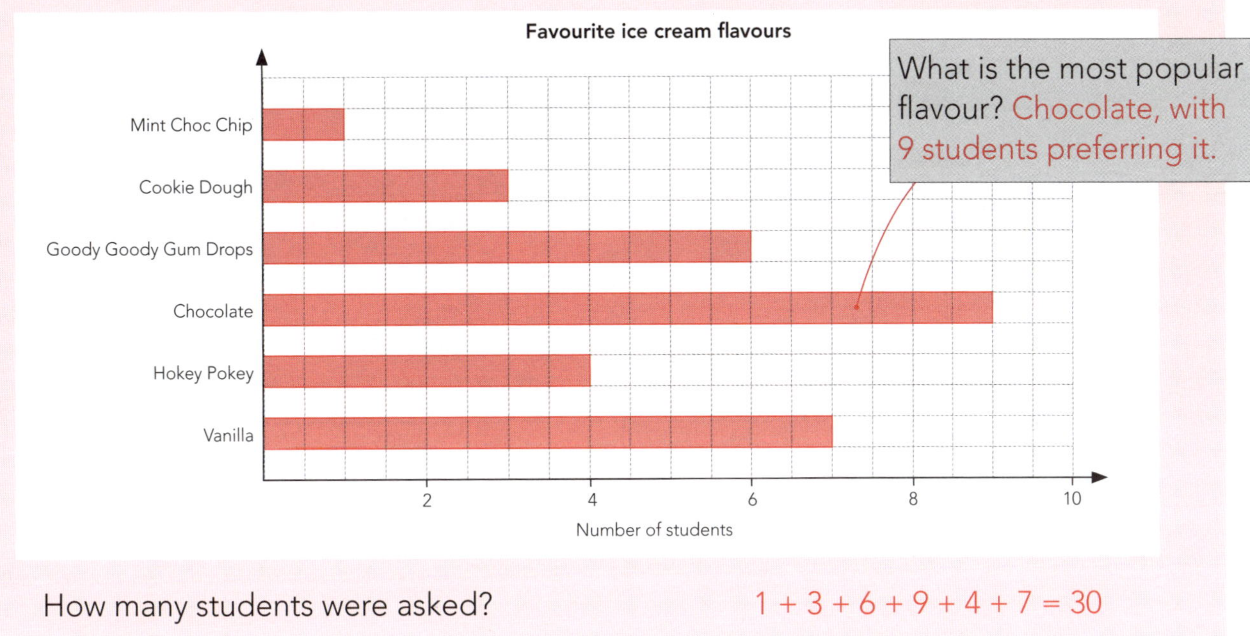

How many students were asked? 1 + 3 + 6 + 9 + 4 + 7 = 30

Answer the following questions.

1 Students were asked whether they thought school blazers should be replaced with a jacket. Here are the results:

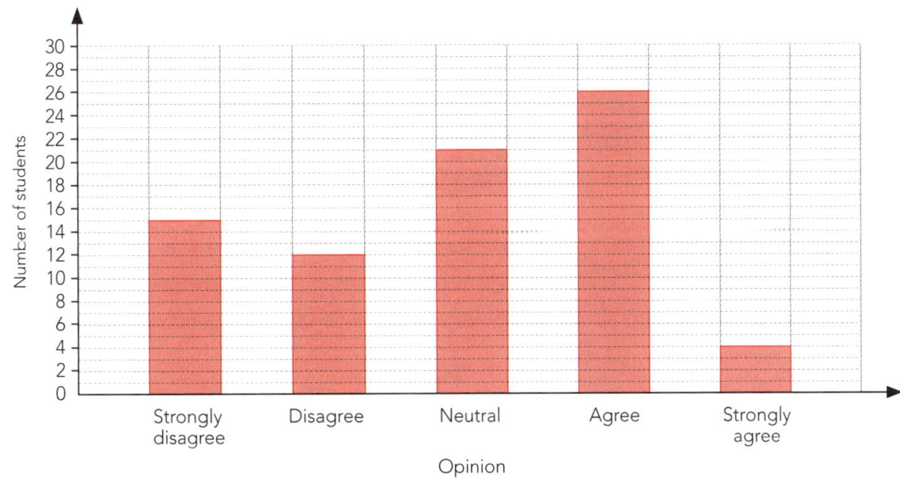

a How many students strongly disagreed? __________

b How many students either agreed or strongly agreed? __________

c How many students were asked about what they thought? __________

d What is the probability that a student strongly disagreed? __________

e What percentage (1 dp) of students either strongly disagreed or disagreed? __________

ISBN: 9780170451420

2 A group of friends voted on which game they should play during lunchtime. Here are the results:

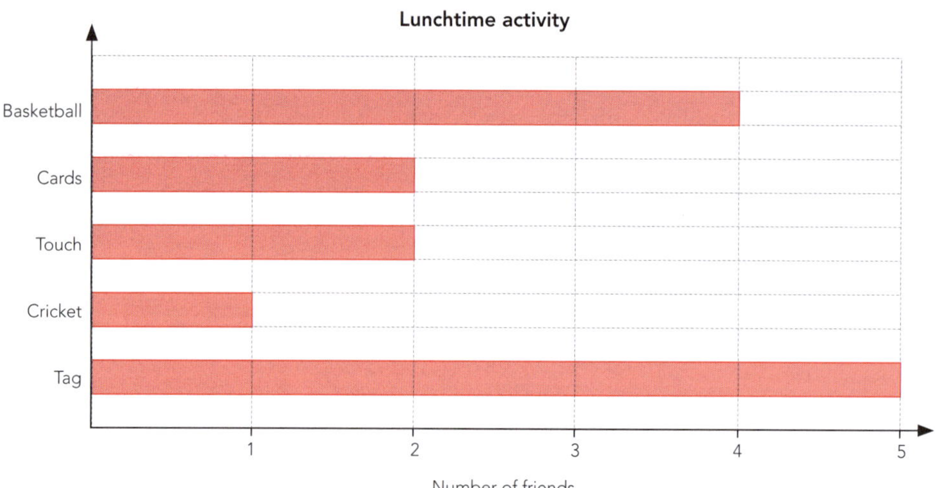

a How many of the friends wanted to play basketball? ______

b How many friends were there in the group? ______

c What is the probability that a friend wanted to play tag? ______

3 The number of detentions for Year 9 and 10 students were recorded for a week.

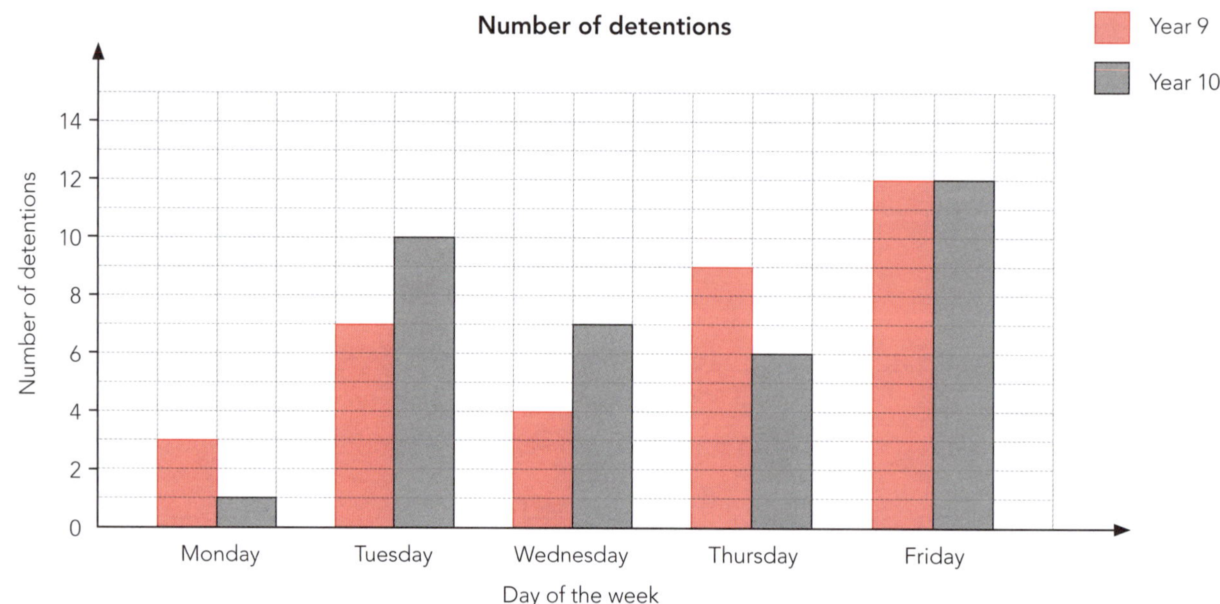

a Which year group had more detentions on a Thursday? ______

b On which day did only one Year 10 have a detention? ______

c Which year group got the most detentions and by how many? ______

 ISBN: 9780170451420

Creating bar graphs

- The bars must all be the **same width**.
- If there is more than one group, there must be a **key**.

Example: Leila counted the colours of lollies in one packet. Here are the results:

6 red, 8 yellow, 3 green, 5 orange, 2 blue, 7 brown.

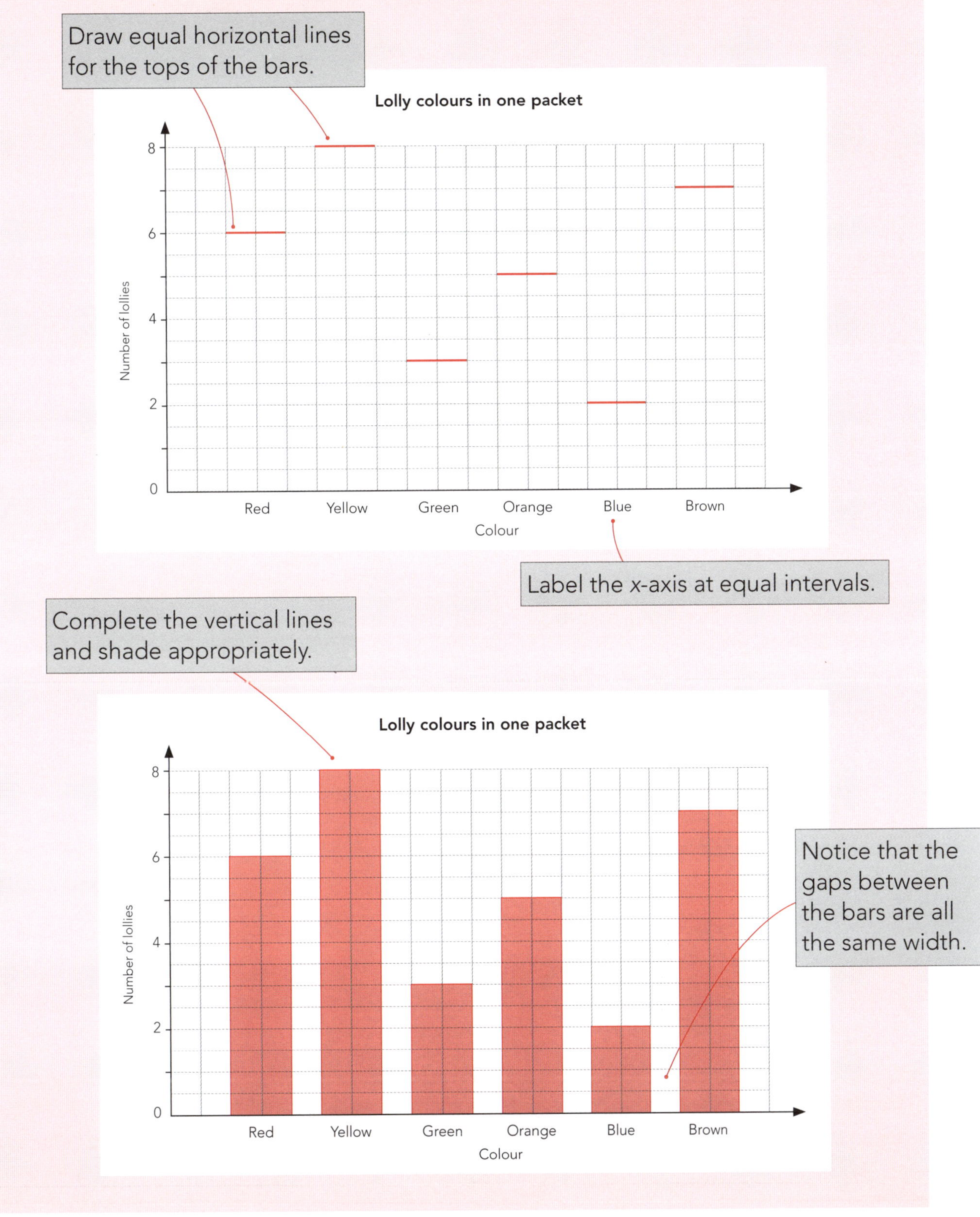

ISBN: 9780170451420

Draw bar graphs for the following data.

4 Hemi tracks how much money he earns each month.

July	August	September	October	November	December
$50	$80	$0	$105	$30	$90

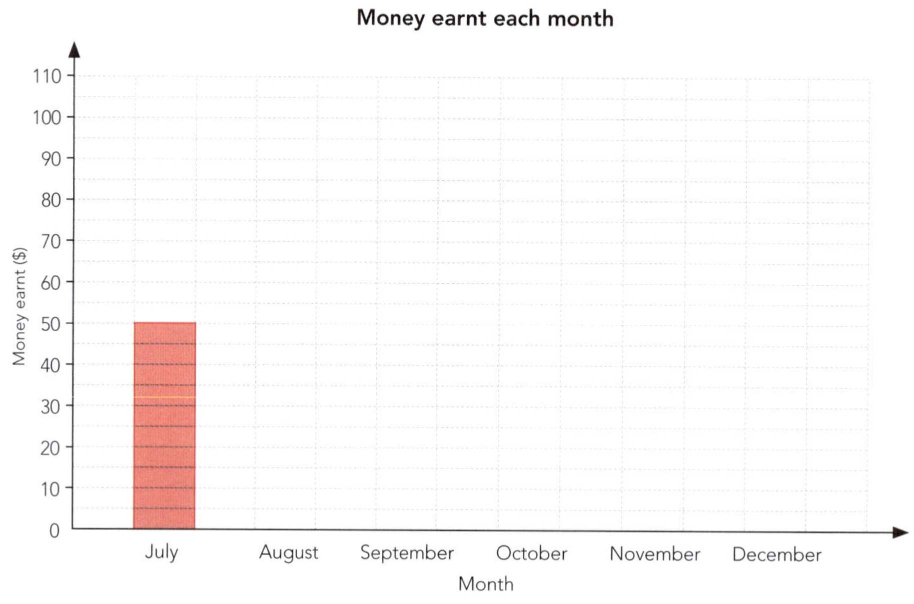

5 Henry had 40 days in the holidays. He spent his time at these locations. Complete the table and the bar graph.

Location	Tally	Frequency
Home	~~||||~~ ~~||||~~ ~~||||~~ ||	
Friend's house	~~||||~~	
Beach	~~||||~~ ||||	
Basketball court		
	Total	

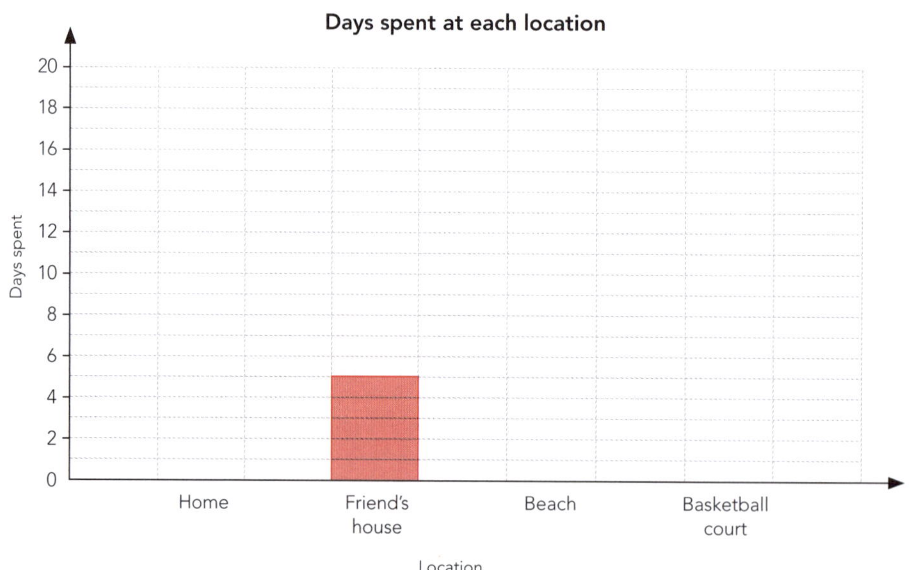

ISBN: 9780170451420

Line graphs

- Line graphs are often used to show how **discrete** or **continuous** data changes at regular intervals of time.
- Lines connect the plotted points.
- Sometimes these are called **time series** graphs.

Understanding line graphs

Examples:

1 Pita recorded how many push-ups she could do each day during the week.

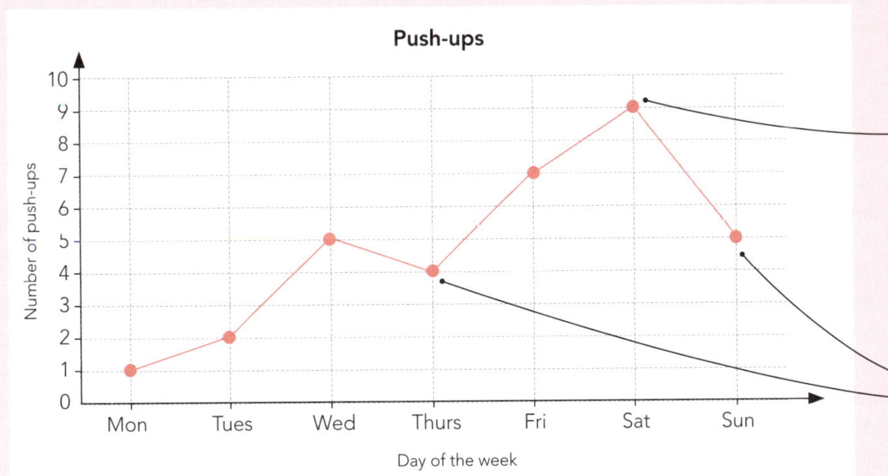

On which day did she do the most push-ups? On Saturday, because that was the highest point with 9 push-ups.

On which day(s) did she do fewer than the day before? On Thursday and Sunday, because the line sloped down to those days.

2 There can be several lines on one graph.
The following week Pita recorded her push-ups and her sit-ups.

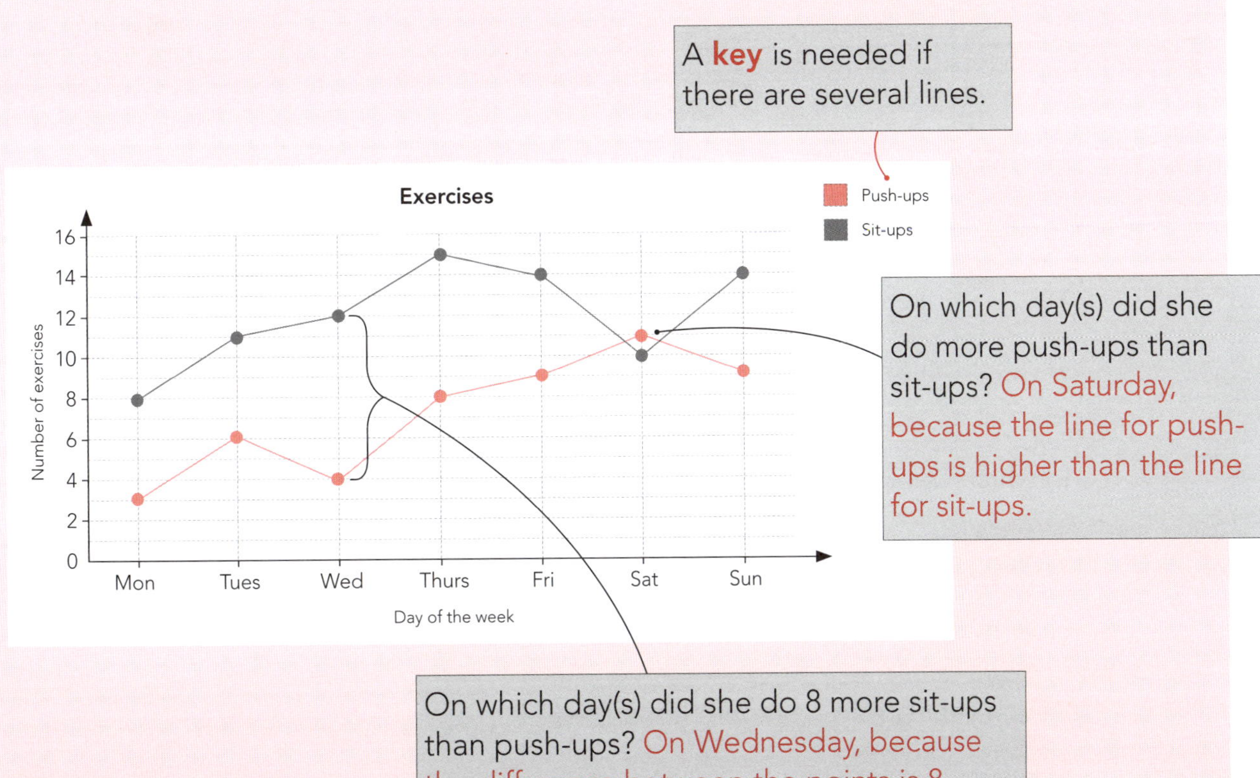

A **key** is needed if there are several lines.

On which day(s) did she do more push-ups than sit-ups? On Saturday, because the line for push-ups is higher than the line for sit-ups.

On which day(s) did she do 8 more sit-ups than push-ups? On Wednesday, because the difference between the points is 8.

ISBN: 9780170451420

Answer the following questions.

1 The school canteen recorded how many pies were sold on each day of the first week of term.

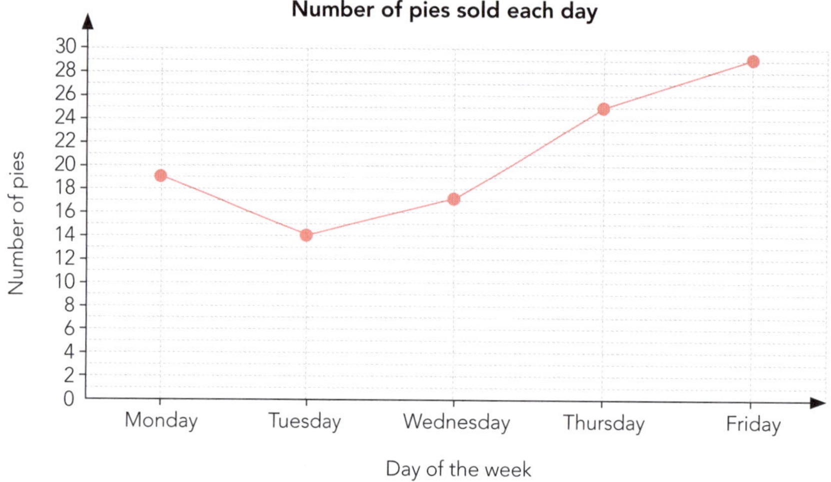

a How many were sold on Wednesday? ____________

b On which day did they sell 8 more than the day before? ____________

c How many pies were sold altogether? ____________

2 A school graphed the absences of Year 9 and 10 students in the first five weeks of the year.

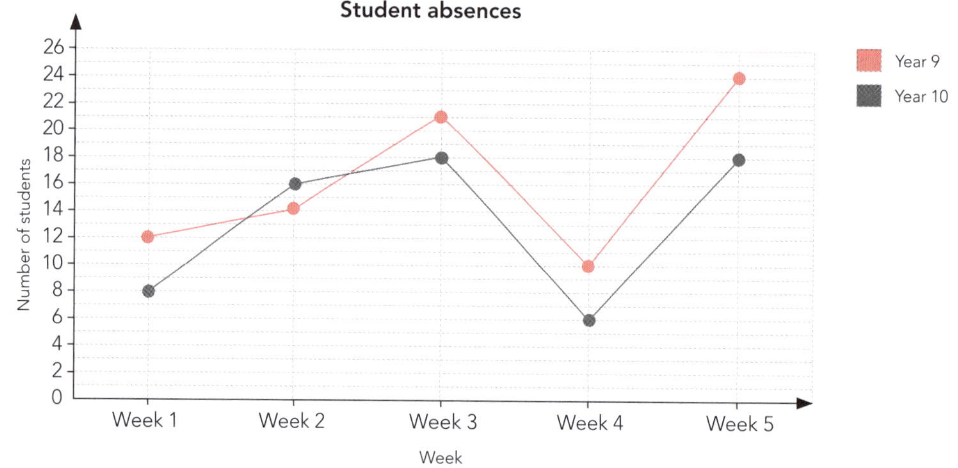

a In which week did Year 10 have more absences than Year 9? ____________

b Which year group had more absences in week 1? ____________

How many more? ____________

c Which year group has more absences? ____________

Explain your answer. ____________________________________

____

ISBN: 9780170451420

Creating line graphs

Example: Maia has been training for a fun run. She has recorded her progress over the first six days.

Friday	Saturday	Sunday	Monday	Tuesday	Wednesday
2.5 km	3.2 km	3.4 km	1.4 km	4 km	3.3 km

Step 1: Plot the points.

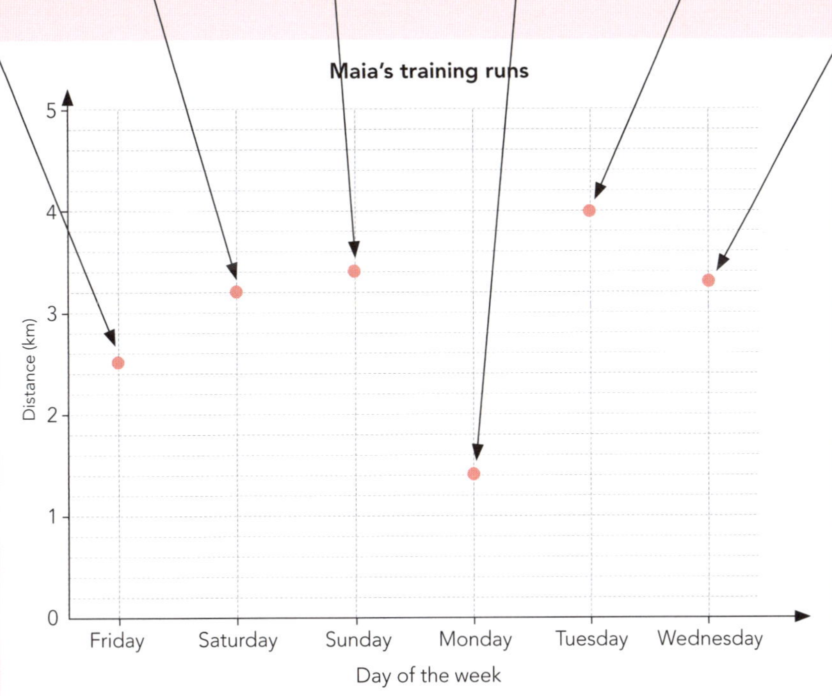

Step 2: Join the points with straight lines using a ruler.

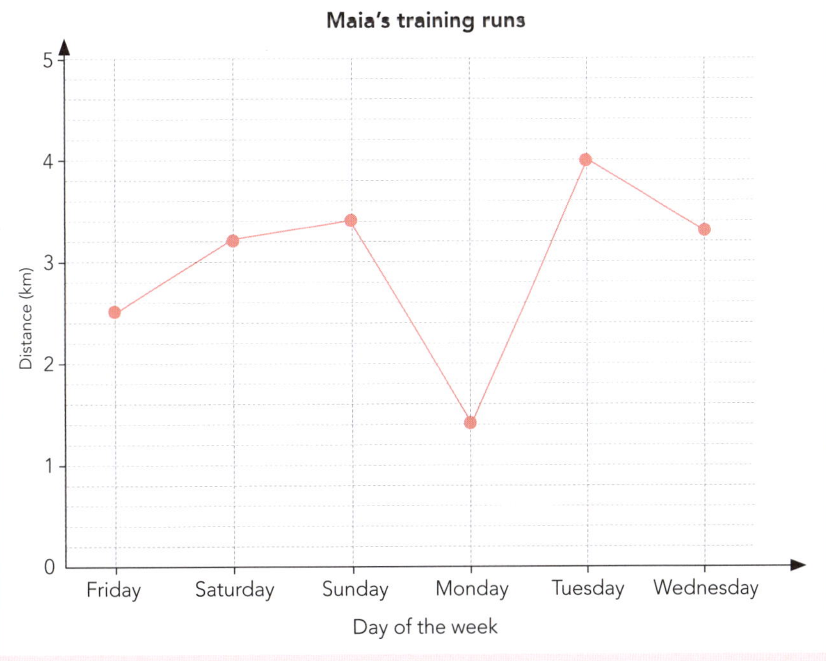

Draw line graphs for the following data.

3 Patrick measured the height of his sunflower (to the nearest 5 cm) at intervals after it germinated.

Day	10	20	40	60	80	100
Height (cm)	5	50	90	105	115	120

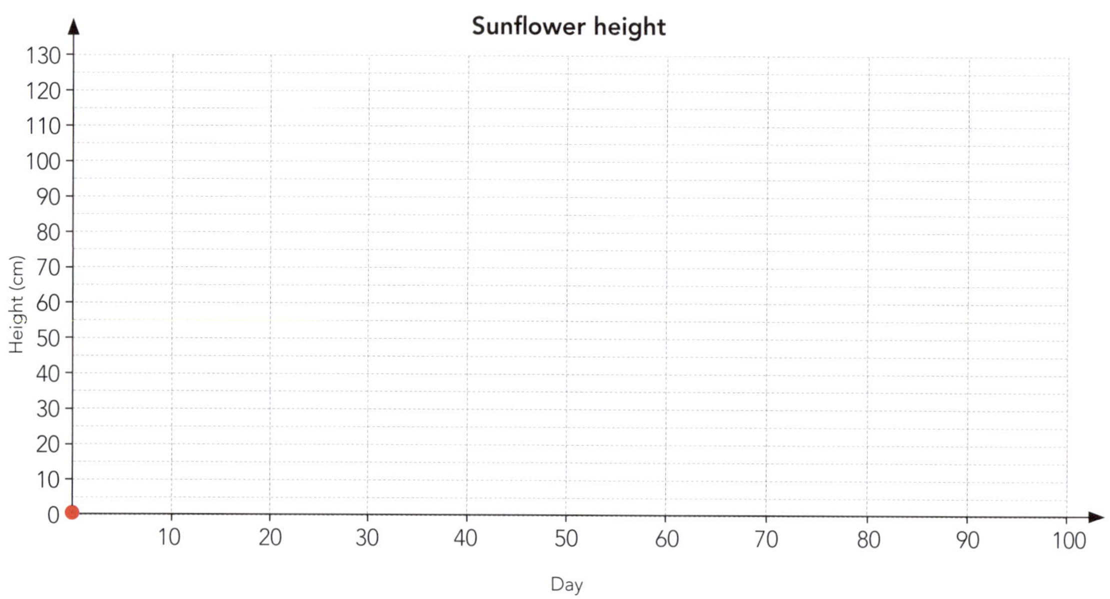

4 Maria sells honey and jam at the local market and tracks how much she earns each week.

Week	**1**	**2**	**3**	**4**	**5**	**6**
Honey	$45	$60	$15	$75	$90	$30
Jam	$10	$25	$40	$55	$45	$35

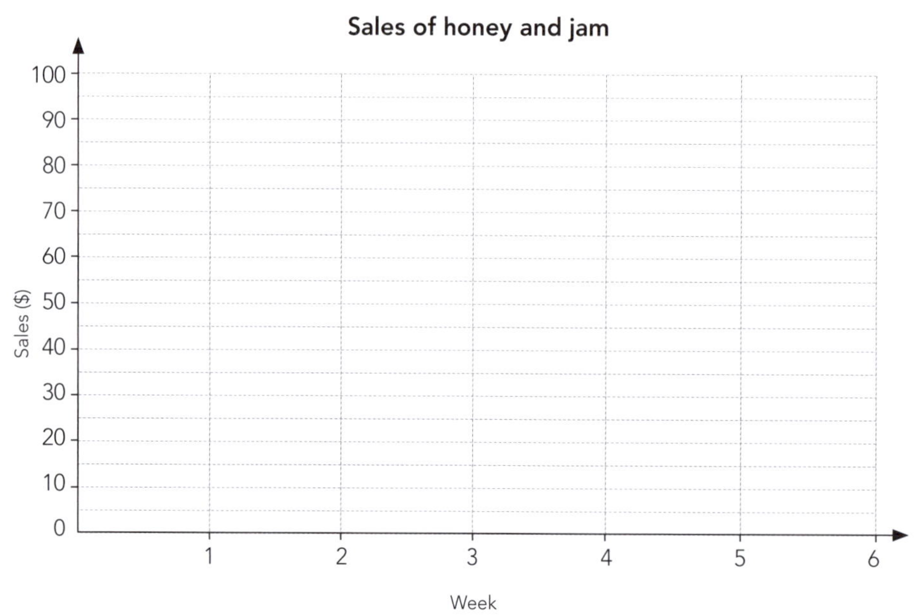

 ISBN: 9780170451420

Histograms

- Histograms are used to display **continuous** (**measured**) data.
- The data is displayed in **intervals**.

Understanding histograms

The heights of students are recorded below.

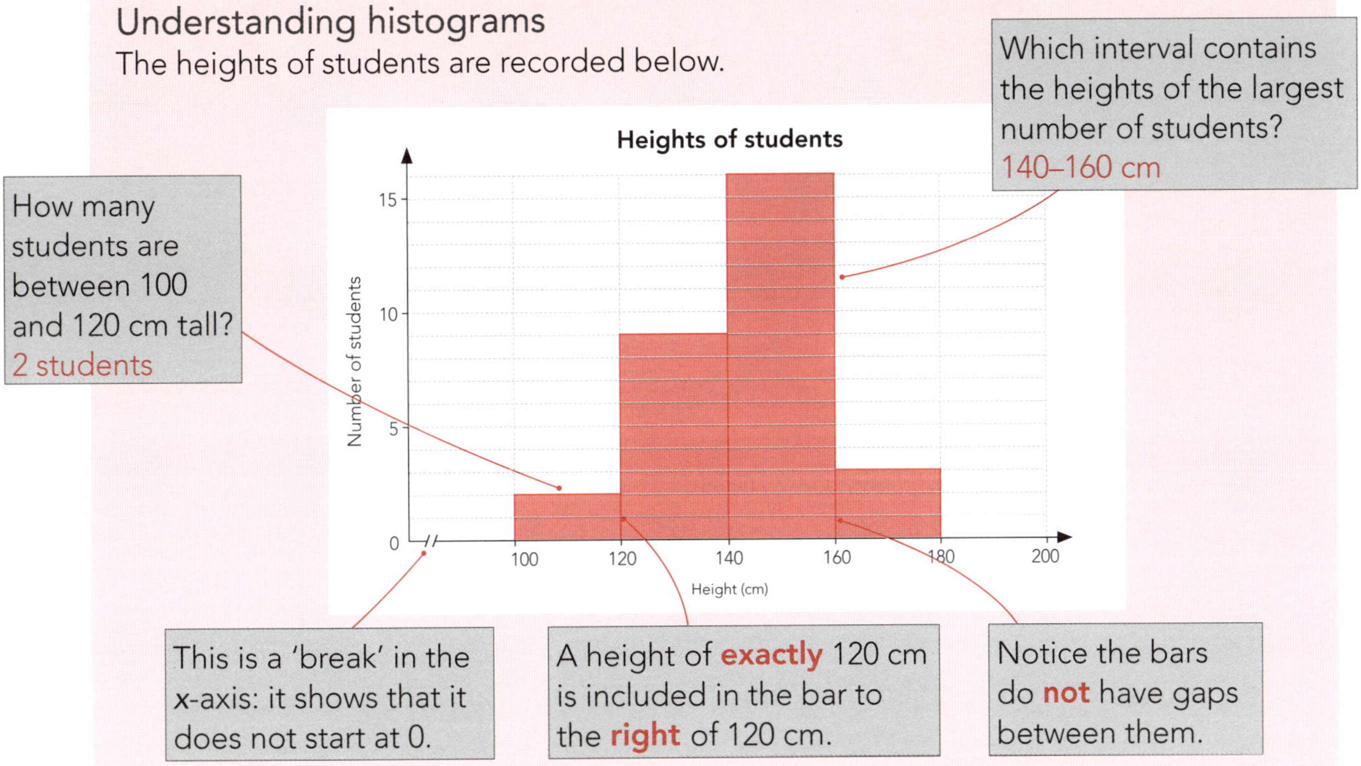

Heights of students

Which interval contains the heights of the largest number of students?
140–160 cm

How many students are between 100 and 120 cm tall?
2 students

This is a 'break' in the *x*-axis: it shows that it does not start at 0.

A height of **exactly** 120 cm is included in the bar to the **right** of 120 cm.

Notice the bars do **not** have gaps between them.

Answer the following questions.

1 Josephine asked the students of her year group how long it took them to get to school today.

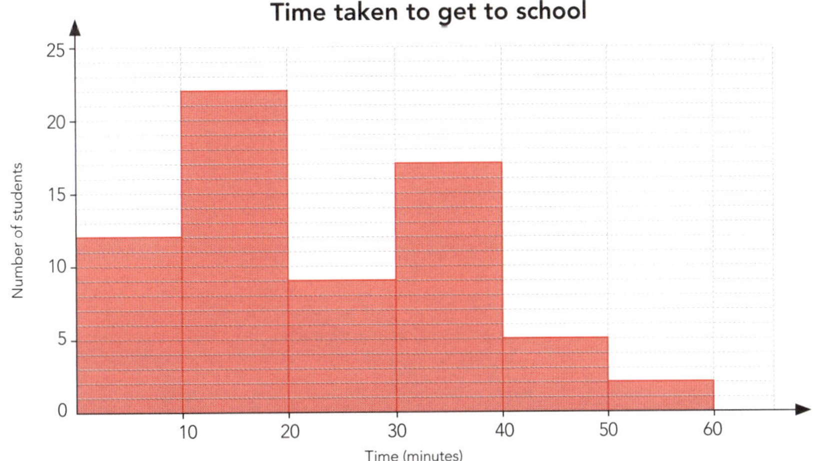

a How many students took between 10 and 20 minutes? ______

b How many students took 30 minutes or longer to get to school? ______

c What fraction of the year group took longer than 40 minutes to get to school? ______

ISBN: 9780170451420

2 Here are the masses of 35 students' school bags.

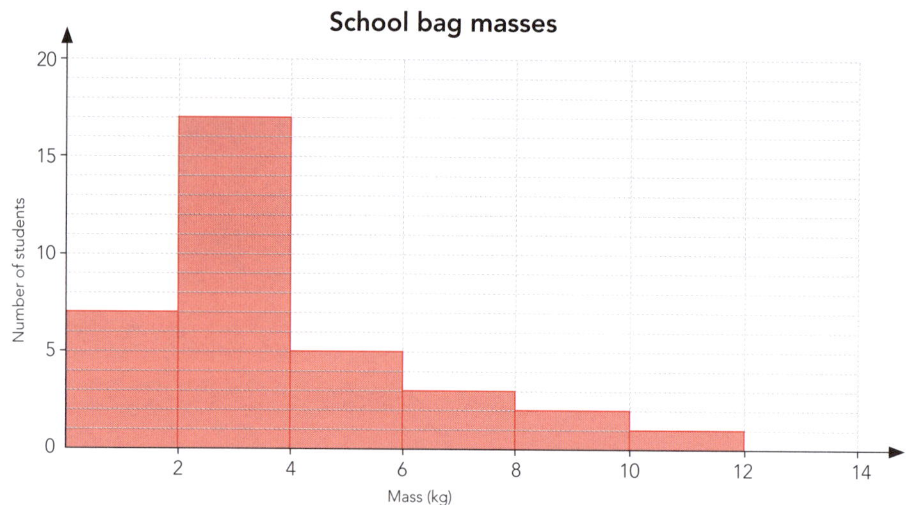

a Which interval contains the largest number of bag masses? ______________

b How many students have bag masses that are less than 2 kg? ______________

c How many students have bag masses more than 8 kg? ______________

d What is the probability that a bag mass was less than 2 kg? ______________

3 Kalani measured the temperature in his classroom during period 1 for each of 31 days.

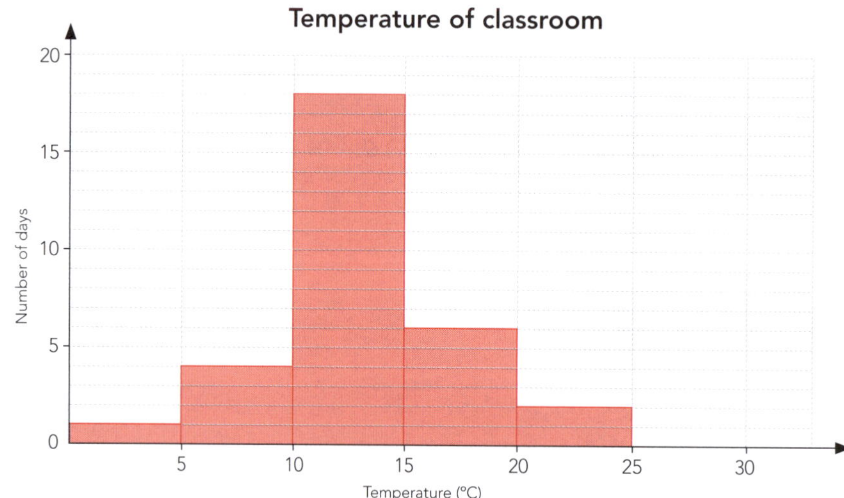

a On how many days was the temperature over 20°C? ______________

b What was the most common temperature range? ______________

c On how many days was it under 10°C? ______________

d On what fraction of the days was it between 10°C and 20°C? ______________

ISBN: 9780170451420

Creating histograms

Here are the hours of sleep students got last night:

Hours	Frequency
0 –	4
4 –	9
8 –	12
12 – (16)	1

'4 –' means these students got **at least 4** hours' sleep and **less than 8** hours' sleep.

'12 – (16)' means this student got **at least 12** hours' sleep and **less than 16** hours' sleep.

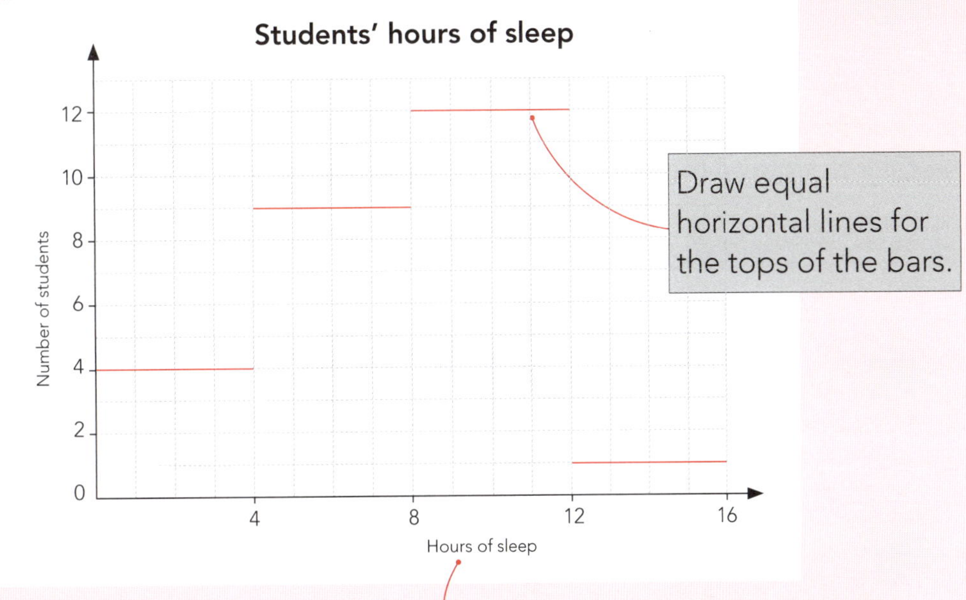

Draw equal horizontal lines for the tops of the bars.

Label the x-axis at equal intervals and write the numbers in line with the **ends** of the bars (unlike bar graphs where they are in the middle).

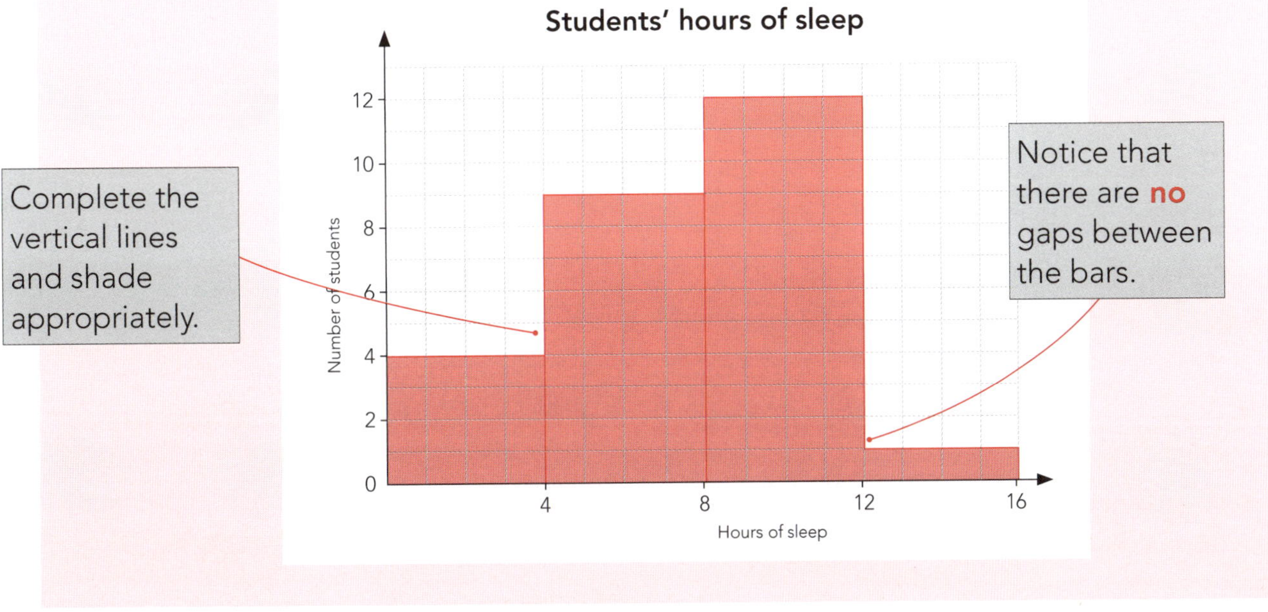

Complete the vertical lines and shade appropriately.

Notice that there are **no** gaps between the bars.

ISBN: 9780170451420

4 A tramping club timed how long it took their members to walk a track. Complete the graph.

Minutes	Frequency
20 –	2
30 –	7
40 –	9
50 –	11
60 – (70)	3

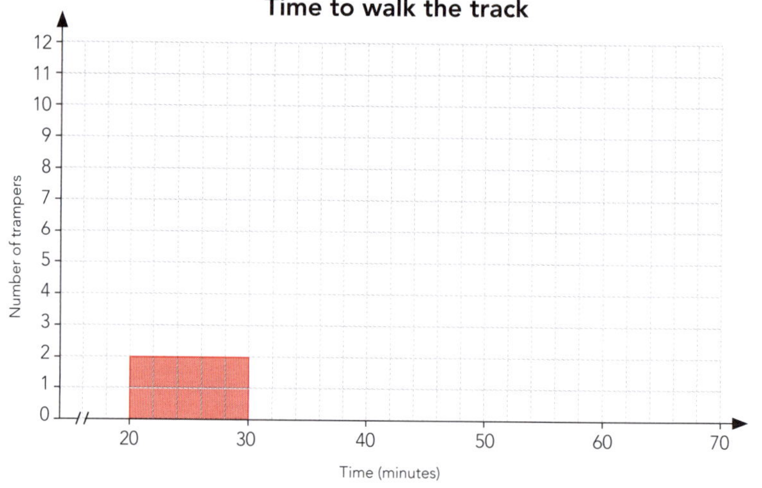

5 Students wrote down how long they spent on homework last night. Complete the tally chart, and then graph the results.

12, 16, 2, 0, 8, 32, 41, 18, 0, 51, 15, 24, 65, 13, 9, 23, 27, 19, 45, 27, 40, 32

Minutes	Tally	Frequency
0 –		
10 –		
20 –		
30 –		
40 –		
50 –		
60 – (70)		
	Total	

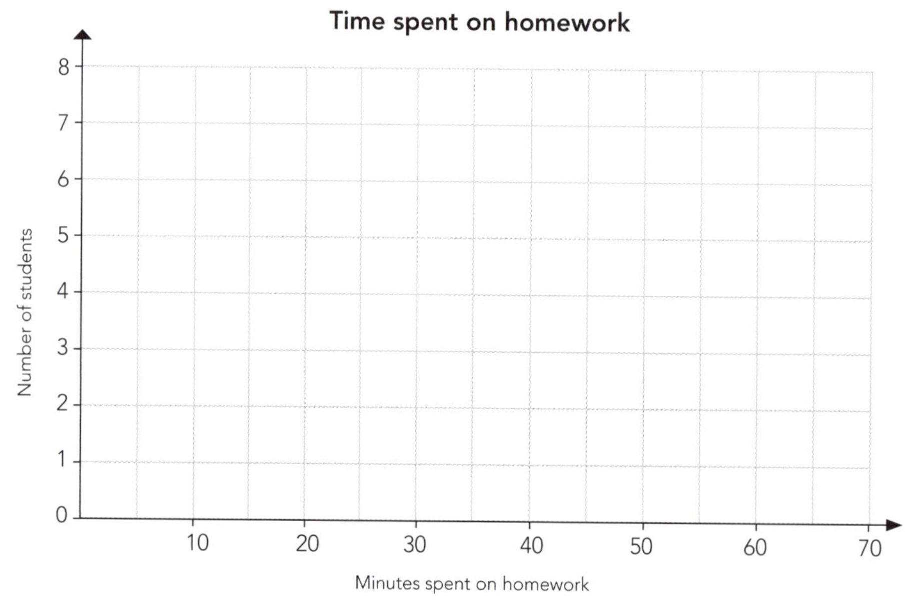

ISBN: 9780170451420

Dot plots

- Dot plots are used for **discrete** and **rounded continuous** data.
- They are useful for **comparing groups**.
- Each dot represents one person/object, unless you are told otherwise.

Understanding dot plots

Examples:

1 Some students were asked how many pets they have at home.

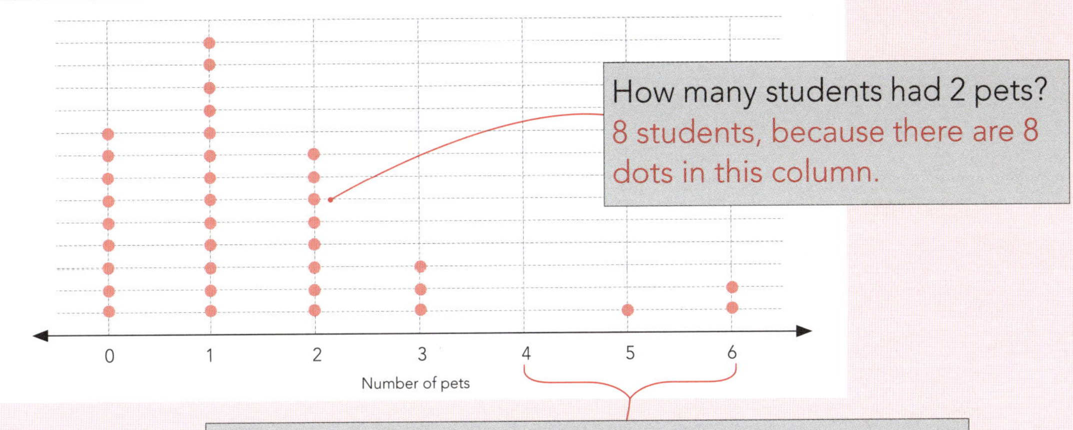

How many students had more than 3 pets?
This means 4, 5 or 6 pets ∴ $0 + 1 + 2 = 3$ students.

Dot plots are useful for comparing data sets.

2 Students kept records of how much time they spent exercising and how long they played video games during the last week.

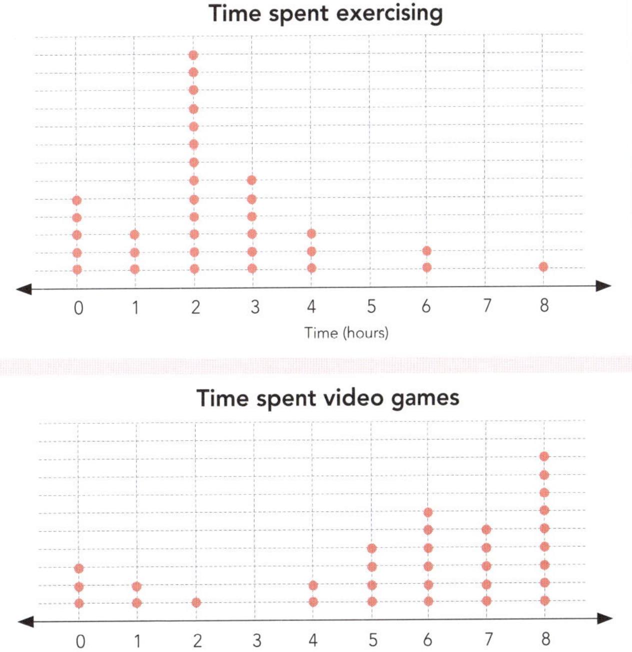

Which activity do students spend more time doing? Playing video games

Explain your answer. There are more dots towards the right of the video game graph, which means that more hours were spent playing video games.

ISBN: 9780170451420

Answer the following questions.

1 Digby asked his classmates how long they spent on homework this week (to the nearest hour).

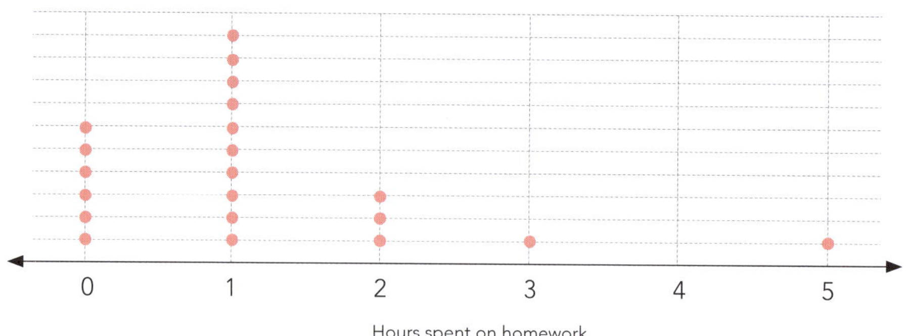

a What is the most common length of time spent on homework? ________

b How many students did less than half an hour's homework? ________

c How many students did Digby survey? ________

d What fraction of his classmates spent at least 1 ½ hours on homework? ________

2 Hamish's class did a science test and a mathematics test.

Science

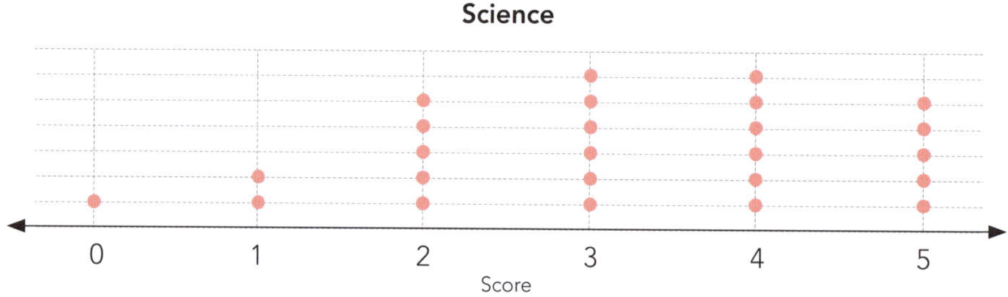

Mathematics

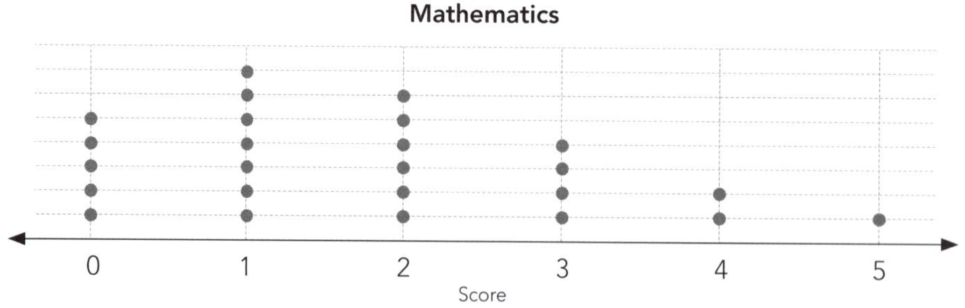

a Which subject did students score better in? ________

b Explain your answer. ____

____

c How many students were in the class? ________

 ISBN: 9780170451420

Creating dot plots

- When creating dot plots, make sure the dots are equal sizes and evenly spaced.

Example: Chloe asked her classmates to write down the names of all the planets they could remember. This is how many they managed:

~~8~~ ~~2~~ ~~1~~ 5 8 7 6 5 5 4 8 5 4 3 7 7 3 6 3 4 3 7 8 5 5 5 3 8 1 0

Cross the values off as you go, to make sure you count each one only once.

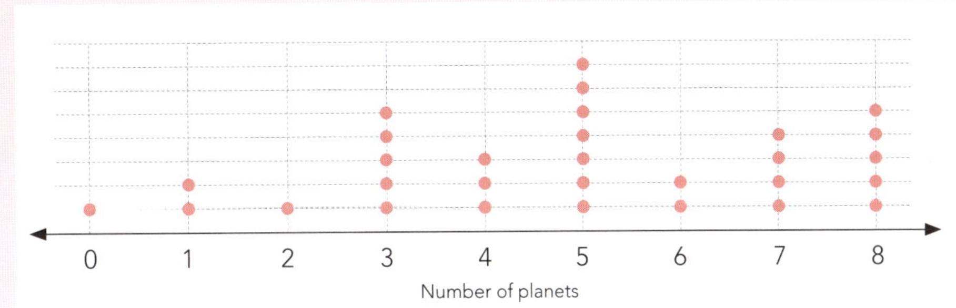

3 **a** Susie asked her classmates to record how many books they read over the holidays. The results are in the table. Add them to the dot plot. The first two have been done for you.

~~2~~	~~3~~	4	0	1	1	3	2	6
2	2	2	1	0	0	1	2	2

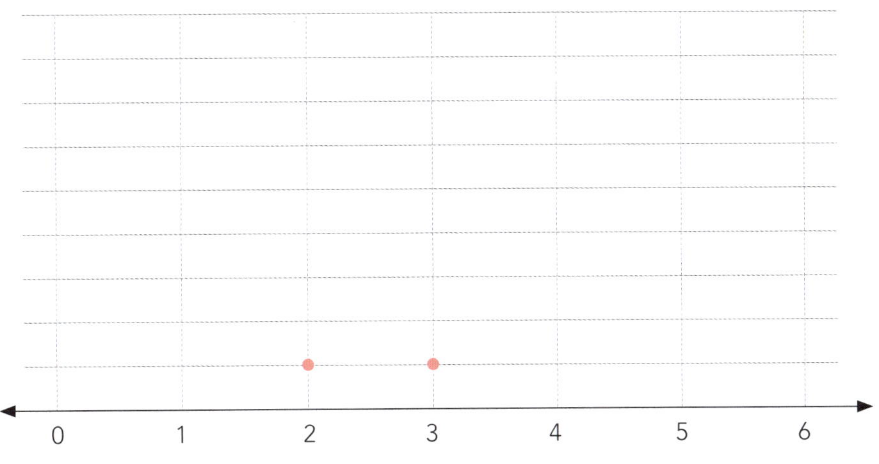

b What fraction of her classmates read no books during the holidays? __________

c What is the probability that a classmate read 2 or 3 books during the holidays? __________

ISBN: 9780170451420

4 Two friends listed the number of goals they scored in each game throughout the season. The results are shown in the tables.

Gerald

2	2	1	3
0	1	4	0
3	1	2	0

Cassie

3	1	0	2
2	3	2	1
0	0	2	1

a Plot the results.

Gerald's goals

Cassie's goals

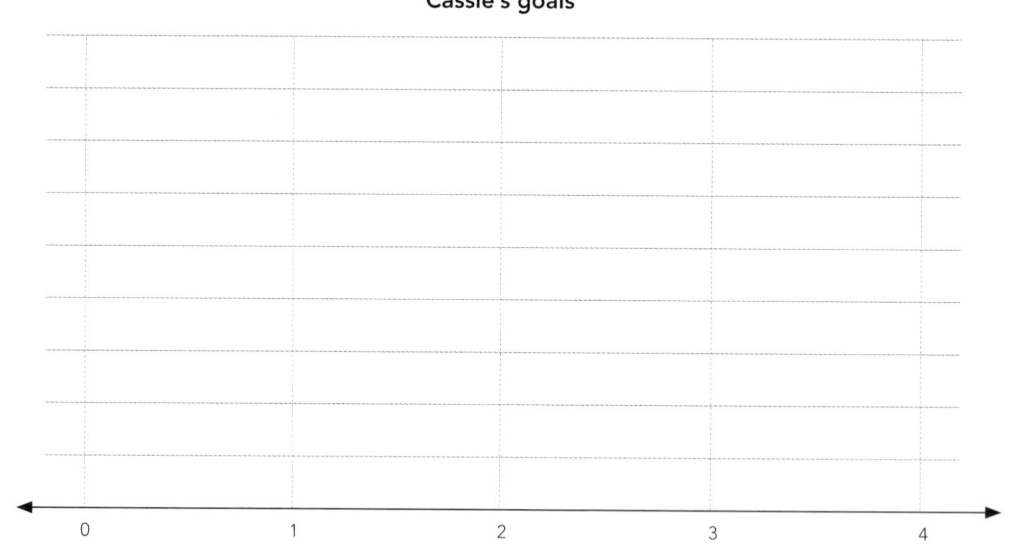

b Gerald is the better player.

☐ Agree ☐ Disagree ☐ Can't tell for sure

Explain your answer. ______________________________

____

 ISBN: 9780170451420

Scatter plots

- A scatter plot is used to show the **relationship** between **two variables**.
- These variables can be **continuous** or **discrete**.
- Each dot represents two pieces of data about one object, e.g. the height and mass of a person.

Coordinate revision

- The **x** coordinate tells you how far to move to the **right**.
- The **y** coordinate tells you how far to move **up**.

Coordinates are written in brackets, in alphabetical order: **(x, y)**.

Examples:

1

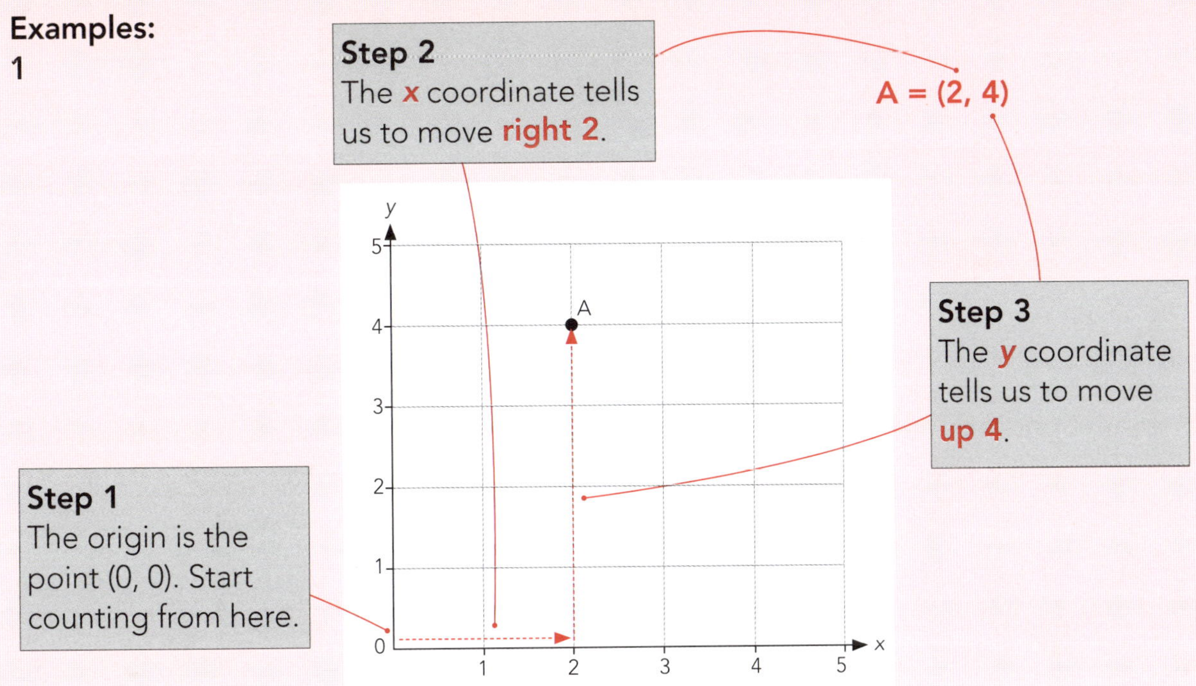

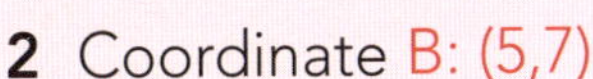

2 Coordinate B: (5,7)

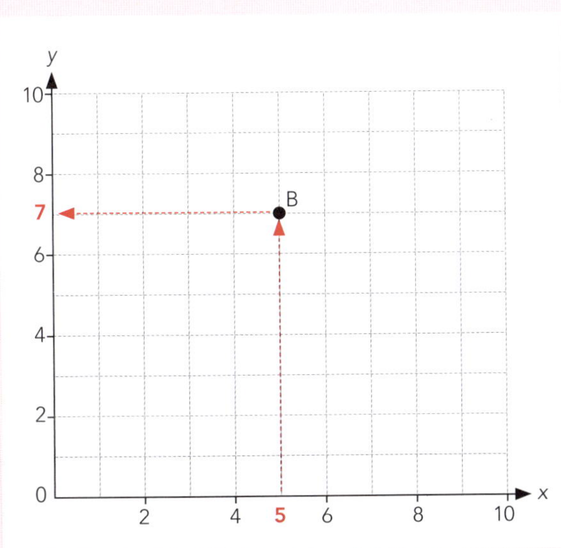

3 Coordinate C: (14,18)

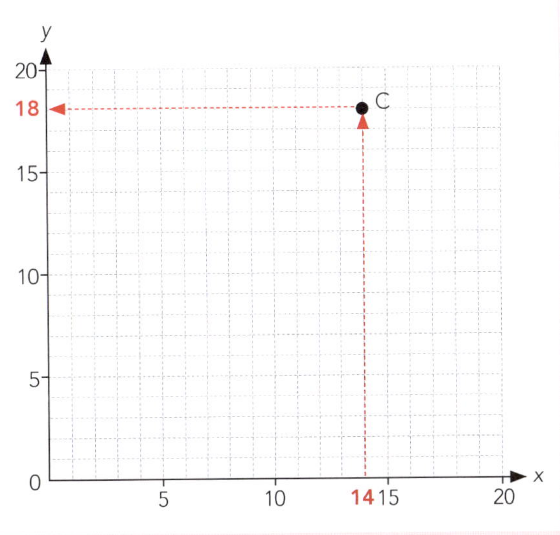

ISBN: 9780170451420

Understanding scatter plots

Examples:

1

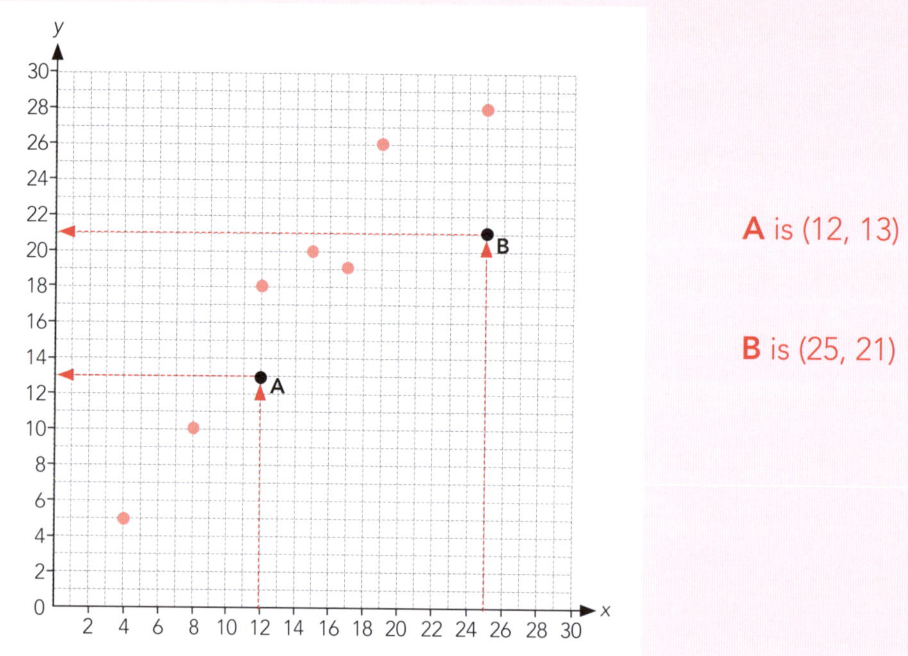

A is (12, 13)

B is (25, 21)

2 The heights and arm spans of a group of students have been plotted below.

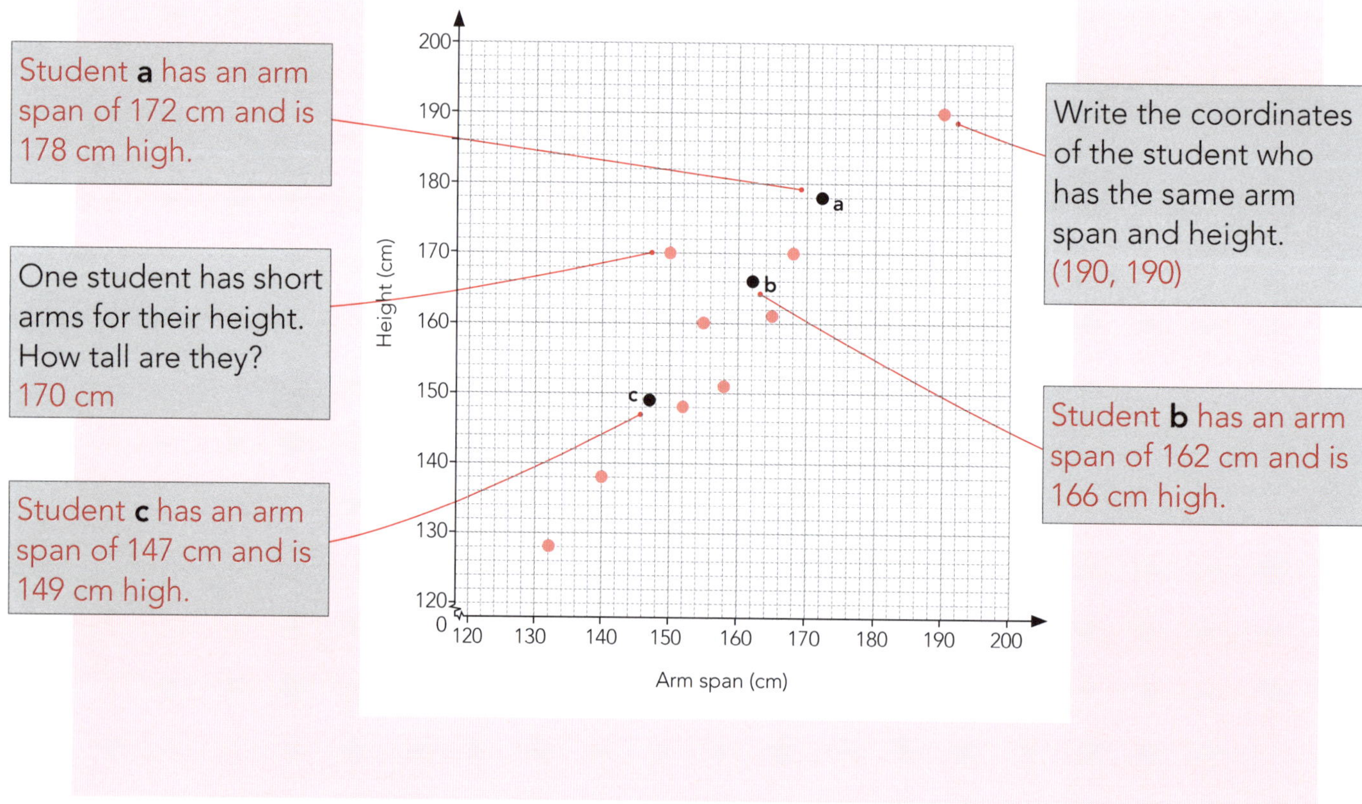

 ISBN: 9780170451420

3 A teacher recorded the time each student spent reading each week, and graphed this along with their mathematics test grade.

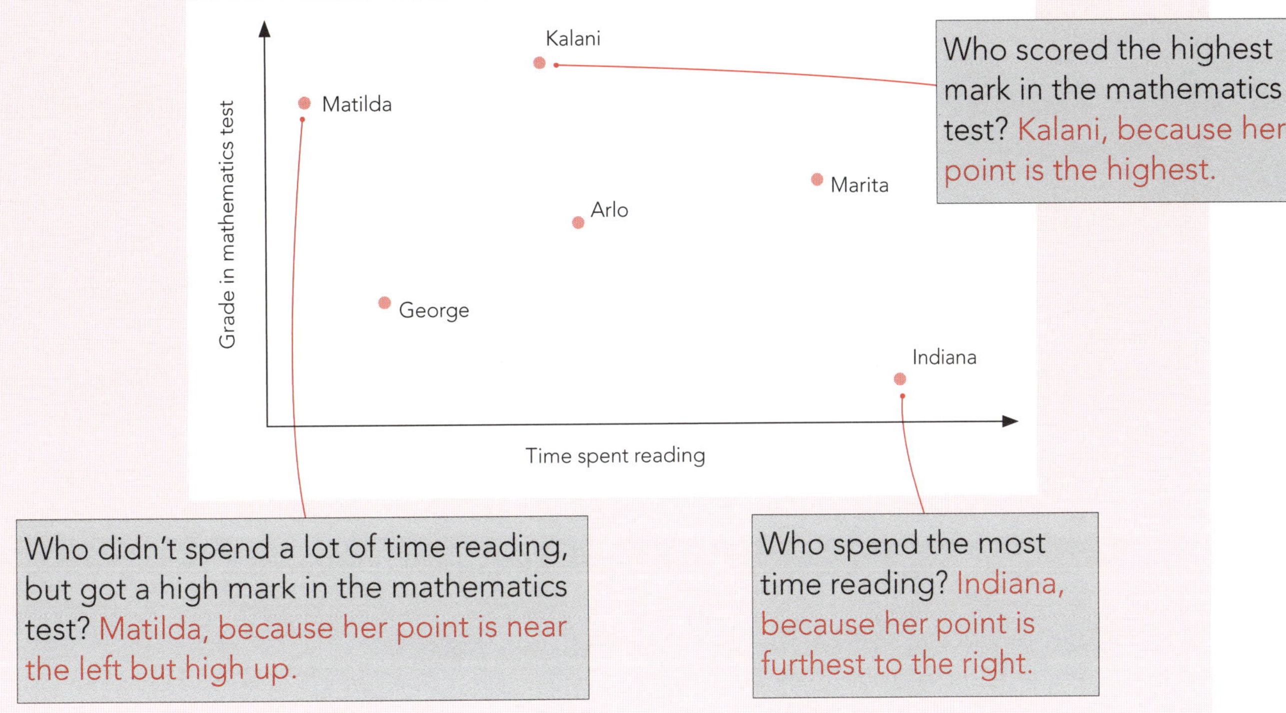

Answer the following questions.

1 Students were asked how long they worked and how much they earnt in the last holidays. The results are plotted on this graph.

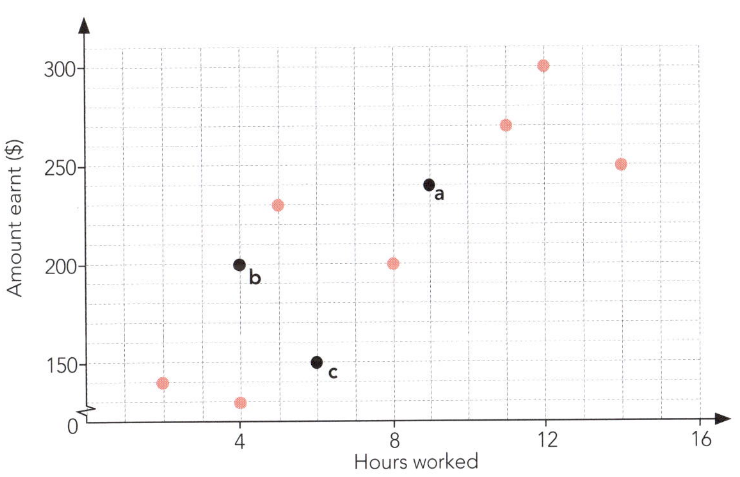

Give the coordinates and description of:

Student	Coordinates	Description
a	(_____, _____)	They worked for _____ hours and earnt $__________.
b	(_____, _____)	They worked for _____ hours and earnt $__________.
c	(_____, _____)	They worked for _____ hours and earnt $__________.

d How many hours did the person who earnt the most work? _______________

e The person who worked the least worked for _______________ hours.

f How much did they earn? _______________

ISBN: 9780170451420

2 Are these statements about the Smith family true or false?

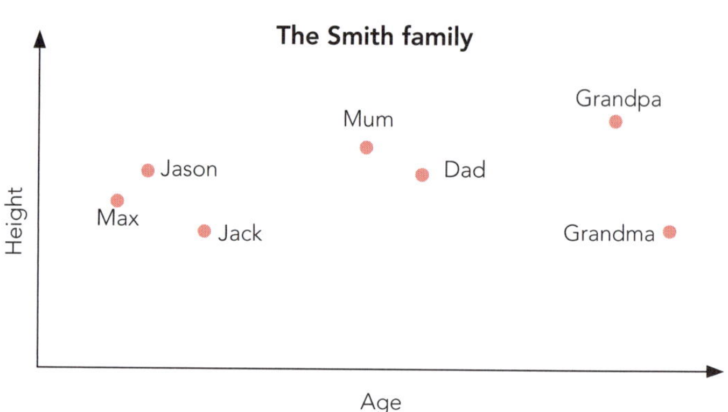

a Grandma is older than Grandpa. True/False

b Mum is taller than Grandma. True/False

c Jack is older and taller than Jason. True/False

d Max is younger and shorter than Jack. True/False

3 Students were asked to measure the distance they travel to school and to find the mass of their school bag.

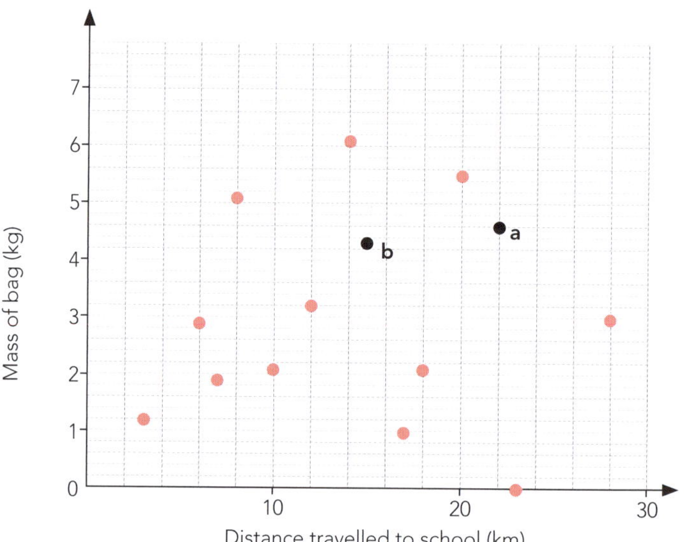

Complete the table.

Student	Coordinates	Description
a	(____, ____)	They travelled ____ km and their bag was ________ kg.
b	(____, ____)	They travelled ____ km and their bag was ________ kg.

Mark and label the points at:

c (18, 3.2)

d (7, 5.8)

e One student didn't bring a bag. How far did they travel to school? ____________

f How heavy is the bag of the student who travelled the greatest distance? ____________

ISBN: 9780170451420

Creating scatter plots

- It's important to make dots big enough so they can be read, but not so big that the values are unclear.

4 Add the data in the table to the scatter plot.

Age	Time
8	6
6	9
12	6
4	14

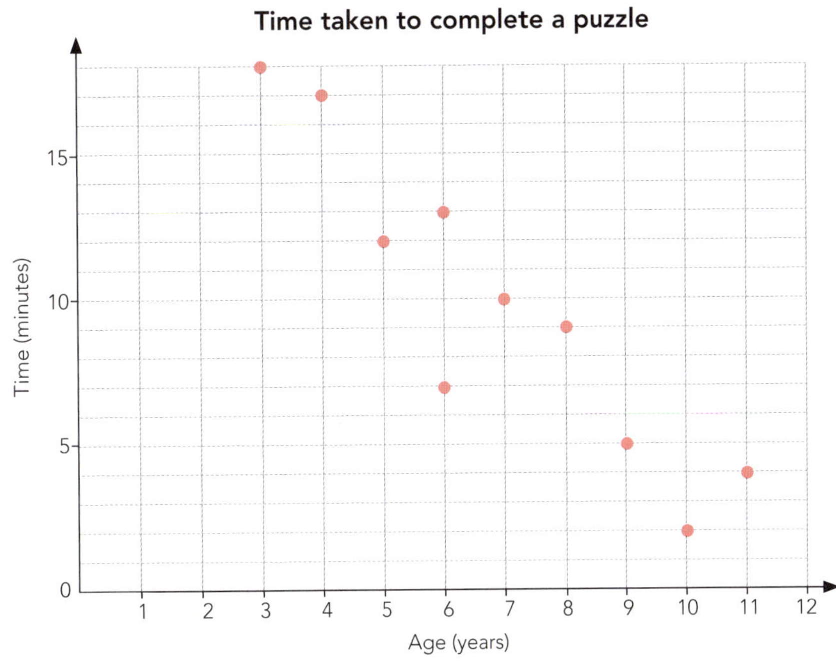

5 Match the names to points x, y and z.

a Courtney got the same grade as Rachel but studied less. __________

b Emanuel studied longer than Vili but he got a lower grade. __________

c Hiroki studied longer than Rachel but less than Vili. __________

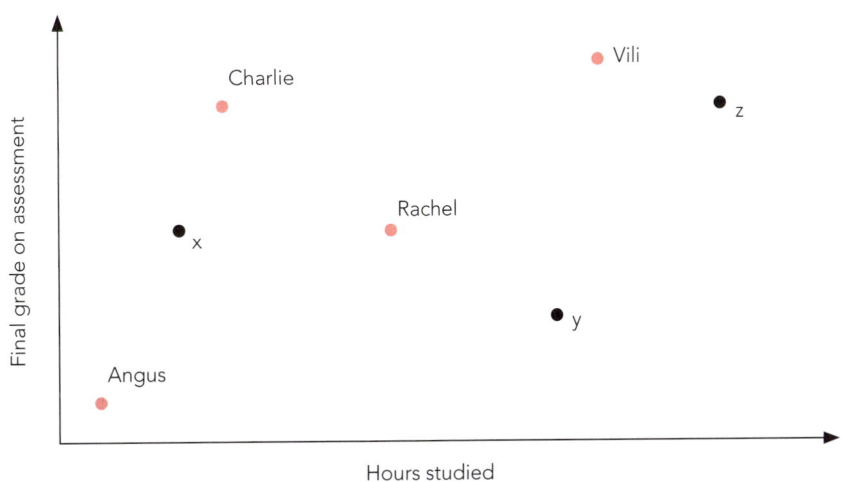

ISBN: 9780170451420

Data analysis

- There are two measures that we need to know in order to be able to discuss and compare distributions:

  1 Where is the **centre** of the data?
  2 How widely is the data **spread**?

Measures of centre (averages)

- There are **three** measures for the centre of data.

Name	Calculation
Mean	$\frac{\text{the sum of all the data values}}{\text{the number of data values}}$
Median	middle value
Mode	value that occurs most frequently

Mean

- The mean is sometimes falsely called the average.
- The numbers do not need to be in order for this calculation.
- Means are often long decimals, so sensible rounding may be needed.
- The mean is influenced by unusually large or small values.

$$\text{mean} = \frac{\text{sum of all the data values}}{\text{number of data values}}$$

Examples:

1 **10 2 9 3 7 6 8 9 9**

$$\text{Mean} = \frac{10 + 2 + 9 + 3 + 7 + 6 + 8 + 9 + 9}{9}$$
$$= 7$$

There are 9 numbers in the data set.

The mean of this data set is 7.

2 **6 3 9 5 0 4 2 1**

$$\text{Mean} = \frac{6 + 3 + 9 + 5 + 0 + 4 + 2 + 1}{8}$$
$$= 3.75$$

Notice that 0 must be included in the calculation.

The mean of this data set is 3.75 or 3.8 (1 dp).

For these data sets, estimate the mean, and then calculate it.

1 **a** **4 5 1 9 8 2 6 7 8 5**

Mean = $\frac{4 + \_\_\_\_\_\_}{10}$

= ______

 ISBN: 9780170451420

b 6 6 4 2 7 9 2 1 0 6 7 3 12

Mean = ______________________

= ________

c 13 17 13 15 19 24 21 9 17 18 20

Mean = ______________________

= ________

d 36 92 41 54 68 35 91 34 86 82 100 40

Mean = ______________________

= ________

Median

- If there is an **odd number of values** in a data, the median is the **middle number**.
- If there is an **even number of values**, the median is **halfway between the two middle numbers** in the data set.
- Before you can calculate the median, you must **put the data in order**.

Examples:

1 A data set with an odd number of values

1 2 3 3 4 6 8 9 9

This is the middle number.

The median of this data set = 4.

2 A data set with an even number of values

2 5 5 6 8 9 9 10

These are the middle numbers. Add them together and divide by 2.

The median for this data set = $\frac{6+8}{2}$ = 7.

3 An unordered data set

~~3 6 1 8 2 3 7 8 1 9~~

Cross them off as you go, to make sure you don't miss any.

Put them **in order** before finding the median.

1 1 2 3 3 6 7 8 8 9

The median for this data set = $\frac{3+6}{2}$ = 4.5.

ISBN: 9780170451420

2 For these data sets, estimate the median, and then calculate it.

a 0 0 1 1 1 2 4 5 6 8 9 Estimate = ______ Median = ______

b 7 7 8 9 12 13 15 17 18 21 22 25 29 Estimate = ______ Median = ______

c 2 3 4 4 5 6 7 8 10 12 15 18 21 22 Estimate = ______ Median = ______

d 4 5 7 9 12 16 17 18 19 23 Estimate = ______ Median = ______

3 Put the data in order, then calculate the median.

a 4 ~~3~~ ~~1~~ 6 8 4 7 9 8 4

1, 3, ______________________________ Median = ______

b 3 12 7 10 7 2 3 7

______________________________ Median = ______

c 4 9 5 8 1 4 10 3

______________________________ Median = ______

d 15 23 21 35 23 28 12

______________________________ Median = ______

4 Find the medians of the following data sets.

a

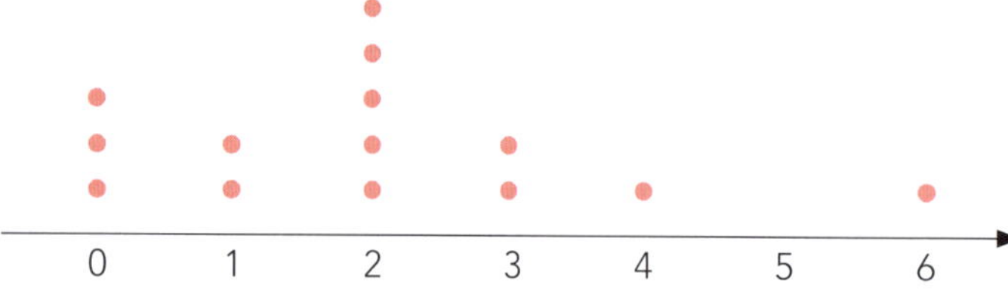

Median = ______

b

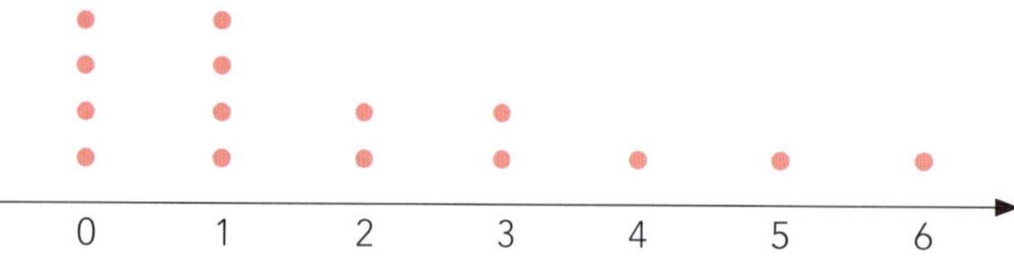

Median = ______

c

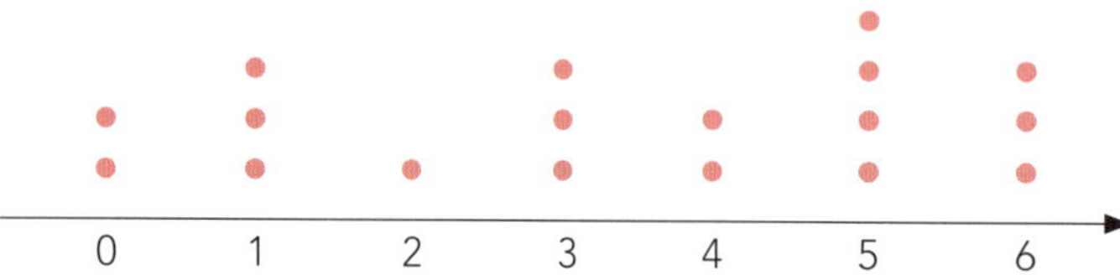

Median = ______

 ISBN: 9780170451420

Mode

- The mode is the **most common value**.
- Sometimes there are **several modes**.
- If there are **three or more** numbers that occur equally often, we say there is **no mode**.

Examples:

1  9 12  5 7  2 4 7 9 10 2  5

The most common number is **3**: there are four of them.

The mode of this data set is 3.

2  2 1   4 5 8  9

Both **5** and **7** occur three times.

The modes are 5 and 7.

3  3 2 5  1 

There are three numbers that occur equally often: **4**, **6** and **2**.

If there are **three or more modes**, we say the data is **polymodal**.

5 Find the mode(s) of these data sets.

a 4 3 1 6 8 4 7 9 8 4 Mode(s) = ______

b 9 12 10 5 9 4 5 10 11 10 Mode(s) = ______

c 21 19 16 14 12 11 21 9 13 14 Mode(s) = ______

d 8 1 2 1 2 6 8 3 2 6 1 0 6 8 Mode(s) = ______

e 4 2 9 6 0 7 3 8 10 11 1 Mode(s) = ______

6 Find the mode(s) of these data sets.

a

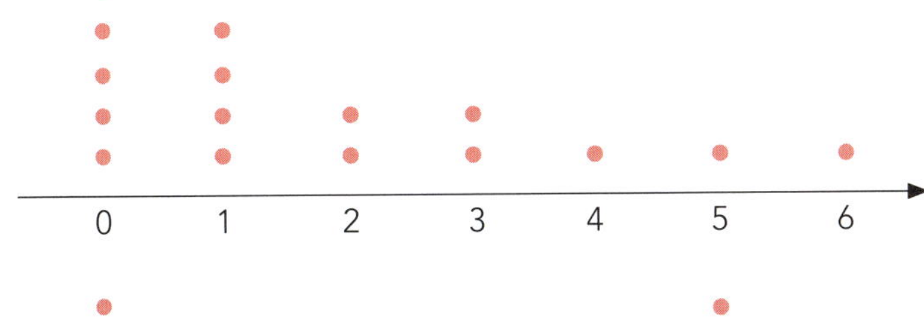

Mode(s) = ______

b

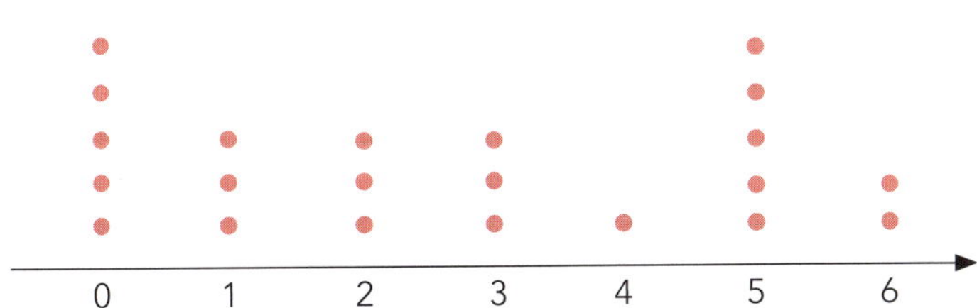

Mode(s) = ______

ISBN: 9780170451420

Measure of spread — range

- The range is the **maximum value minus the minimum value** in the data set.
- Note: the range is a **single number**.
- Like the mean, the range is affected by unusually large or small values.
- The data does not need to be in order to calculate the range.
- The range is a measure of the **variability** of the data.
- Calculating the range for several data sets can help us decide **which is more spread out**.

Range = maximum – minimum

Examples:

1 **10 2 14 5 7 3 9 11 18 3 9 6**

The smallest value in the data set (minimum).

The biggest value in the data set (maximum).

Range = 18 – 2
= 16

The range or the spread of this data set is 16.

2 Two classes took the same test this week. There were 10 questions. The table shows the results.

9A	5	8	7	6	2	5	3	**1**	7	7	4	8	1	3	2	4	9	2	6	**10**
9B	5	8	6	6	7	4	6	5	5	7	6	7	**8**	4	4	5	6	6	6	**3**

9A: Range = 10 – 1
= 9

9B: Range = 8 – 3
= 5

∴ 9A has a larger range (9) than 9B (5), so the test results for 9A are more variable.

Answer the following questions.

1 Calculate the range for the following data sets.

a **6 3 1 7 7 4 7 9 8 4** Range = ______________

b **15 21 54 23 14 17 82 39 12 19** Range = ______________

2 **a** The biggest number in a data set is 15, the range is 12. Smallest number = __________

b The smallest number in a data set is 23, the range is 56. Biggest number = __________

3 Two other classes took the same test. The table shows the results.

9C	5	8	7	6	2	5	3	2	7	7	4	8	8	3	2	4	9	2	6	10
9D	5	8	6	6	7	4	6	5	5	7	6	7	8	4	4	5	6	6	6	3

Which class had more variable results?

9C: Range = _____ – _____
= _______

9D: Range = _____ – _____
= _______

∴ 9____ has a larger range (____) than 9____ (____), so the test results for 9____ are more variable.

 ISBN: 9780170451420

Unusual features

- There are two unusual features to watch for: **unusual points** or **clusters**.
- An unusual point is one that is away from the rest of the data.
- A cluster is a group of data that is away from the rest of the data.

How many make a cluster?
Don't get hung up on labels and definitions; it's best to write what you see. If there are two points away from the rest, then say that.

Examples:

1 Heights of Year 9 students in cm: **156 148 171 168 165 215 149 157**

This student's height (215 cm) is 44 cm more than the next tallest student (171 cm). So 215 cm is an unusual point.

2 It is often easiest to see unusual points and clusters when the data is graphed.

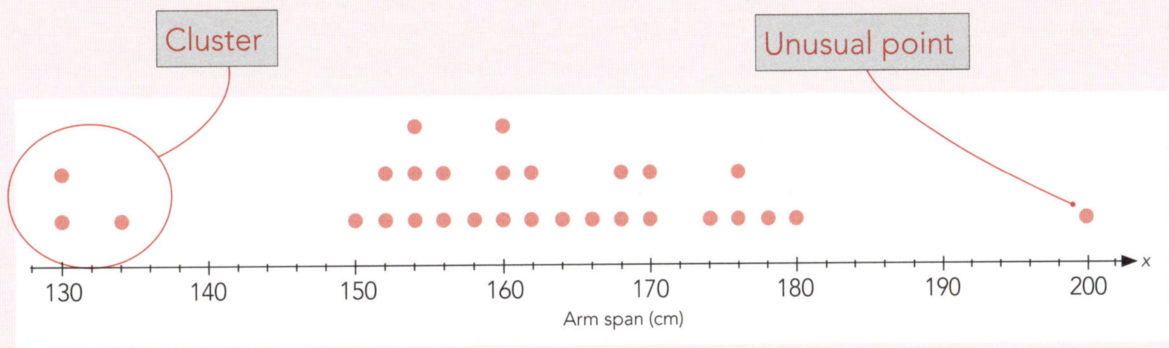

Note: 1 Check that unusual points are not mistakes in measurement, counting or recording.
2 Include them when you graph and analyse your data. Think about whether the unusual feature is possible and state your thoughts when you discuss the data.

Circle or highlight any unusual features in these data sets and state whether they are clusters or unusual points.

1

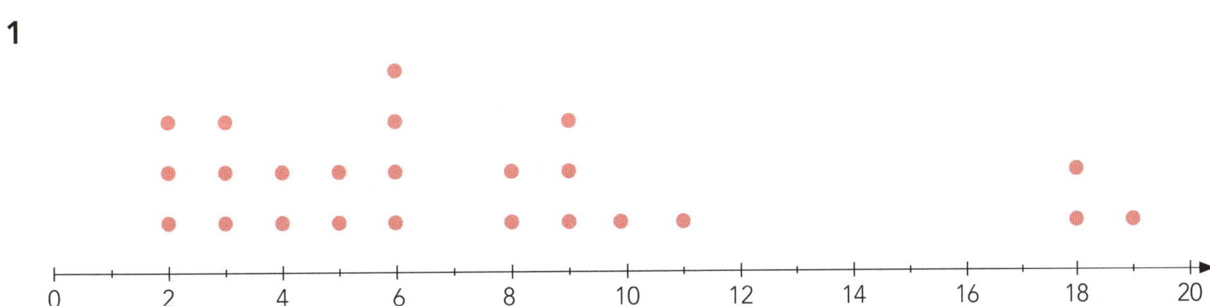

2

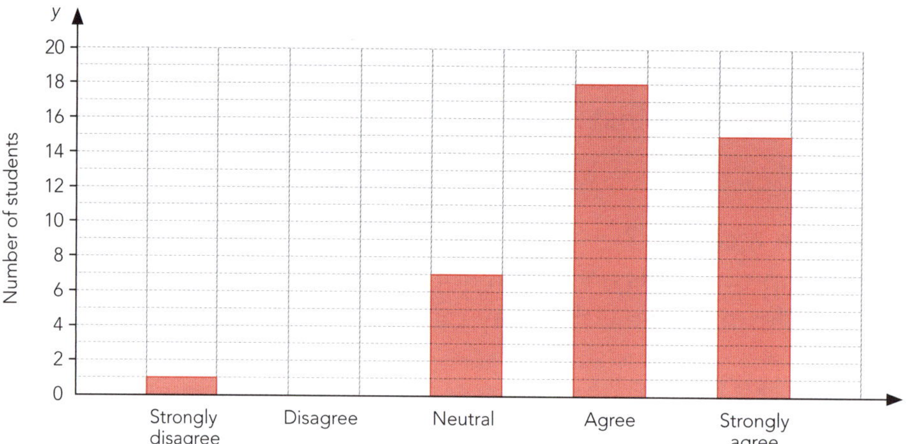

3

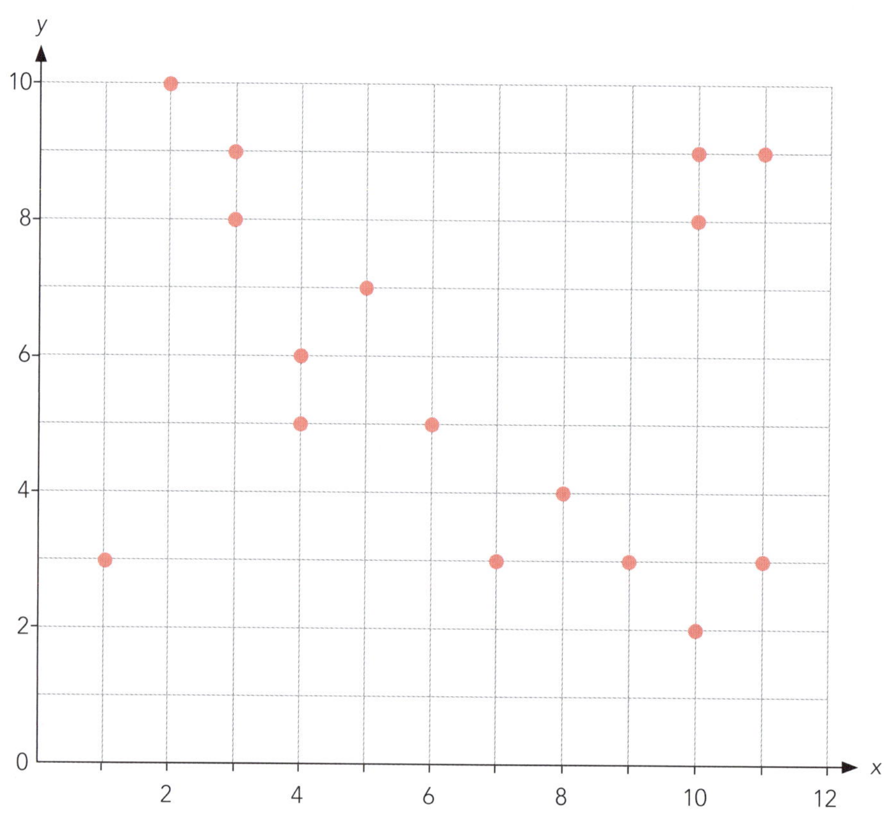

4 Test marks out of 20:

15 18 12 16 19 20 15 14 3 10 16 14 18

5 Number of siblings:

0 3 2 1 0 1 1 2 9 2 1 0 4 2 3

 ISBN: 9780170451420

Statistical literacy

Statistical literacy is about:

- deciding whether a sample or survey has been done **fairly**
- identifying appropriate ways to display data **fairly**
- **being critical** about what you see or read
- **justifying** conclusions based on data and displays.

Sampling and bias

Sample size

- Each sample needs to be **large enough** to ensure that it reflects the characteristics of the population.
- As a loose guide, around 10% of the population is considered a reasonable number.
- However, time, cost and convenience need to be considered when deciding sample size.
- The larger the sample size, the more closely it is likely to reflect the population.

Sampling method

- It's important that the survey captures responses that are **representative** of the population.
- If a sample isn't representative of the population, then we say it is **biased (unfair)**.
- **Bias** occurs when the results reflect one group of the population.
- A **biased** sample **is not truly representative** of the population.

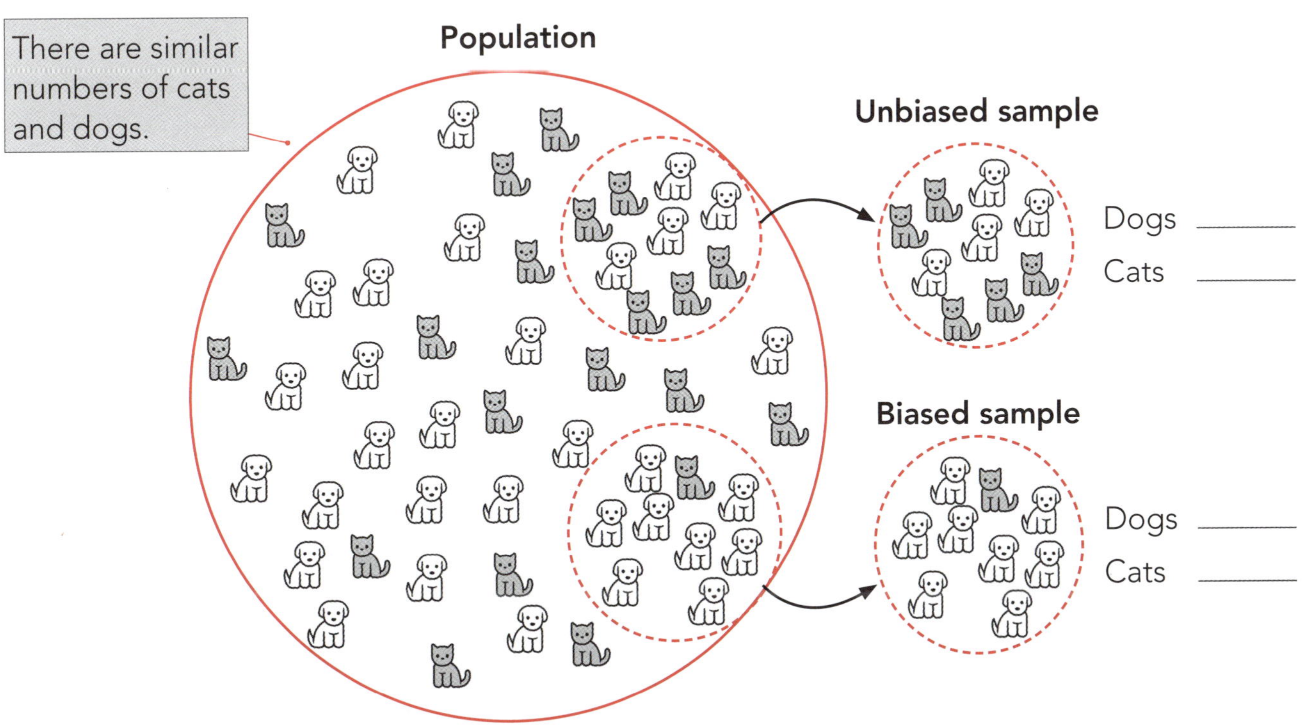

ISBN: 9780170451420

For these situations, is the sample size adequate or inadequate? Is the sample fair or biased?

	Situation	Big enough sample?	Fair or biased?
1	Asking the first 5 students to get to class about whether they have completed their homework or not.		
	Why?		
2	Surveying 50 Year 9 boys at a co-ed school about what music they want at the school disco.		
	Why?		
3	Asking every tenth student on the Year 9 roll surveyed about what music they want at the disco.		
	Why?		
4	Asking 25 students at the canteen if they want to see school ties made compulsory.		
	Why?		

Explain why these samples are likely to produce biased (unfair) results.

5 A group of students sitting together at lunch were asked about their preferences for school uniform.

____

6 A random selection of people were called on their cellphones at 11 a.m. for a survey on free internet.

____

7 A current affairs television programme asked people to vote for their opinions on vaccinations via text.

____

8 People in the mall were asked what they think of the current Prime Minister.

____

9 The members of the netball team were asked whether they thought PE classes should be compulsory at Year 11.

____

ISBN: 9780170451420

Recognising unfair data displays

- Sometimes, published graphs are misleading or incorrect.
- This may be intentional or careless. Either way, it pays to think carefully about the information and who presented it.

Some common tricks

1 Making graphs 3D

a 3D pie graphs

Wedding guests were asked which meal they would like.

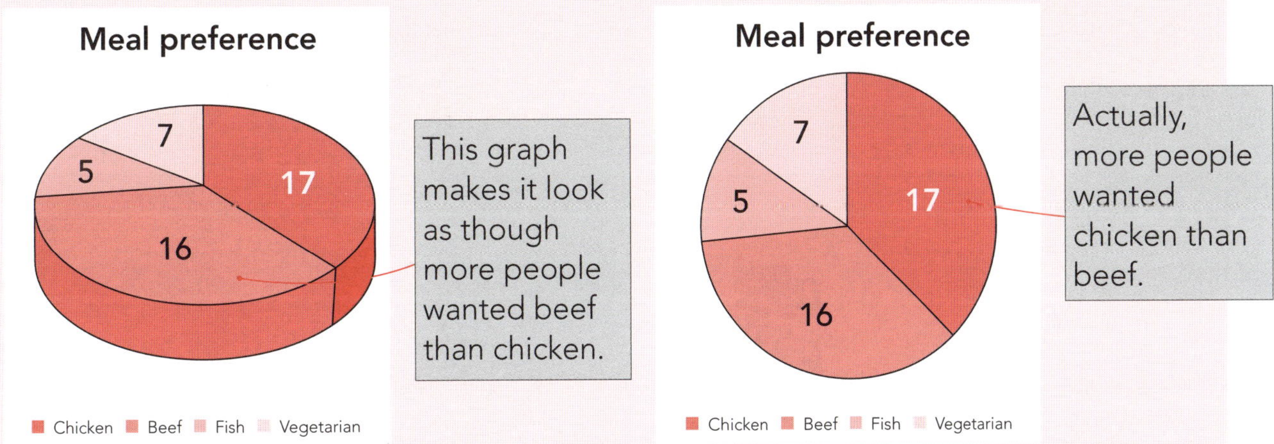

These are misleading because the **sector at the front always looks bigger than it should**.

b 3D bar graphs that use perspective

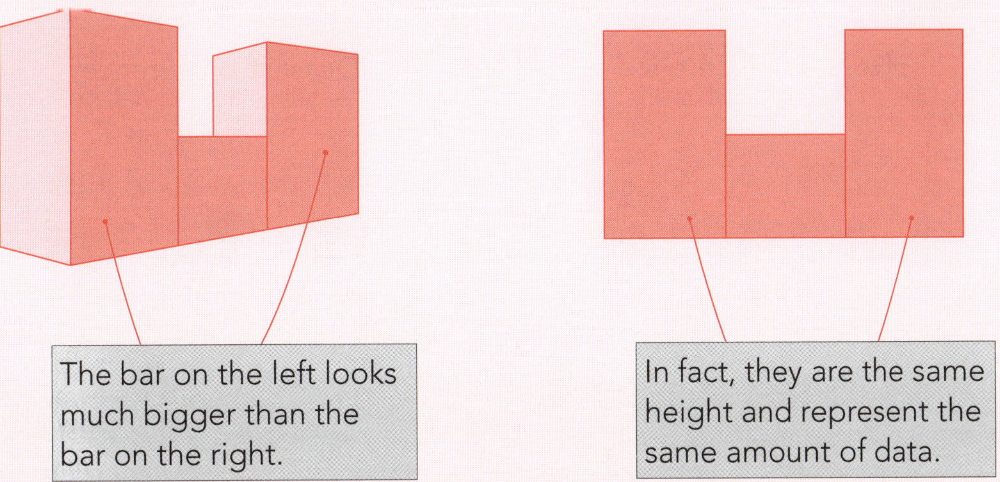

These are misleading because they **make the bars look bigger or smaller, depending on which is 'closer'**.

ISBN: 9780170451420

2 Pictographs with scaling of 2D images

Aroha recorded the number of trucks through two different intersections. She found that there were three times as many going through intersection B compared with intersection A.

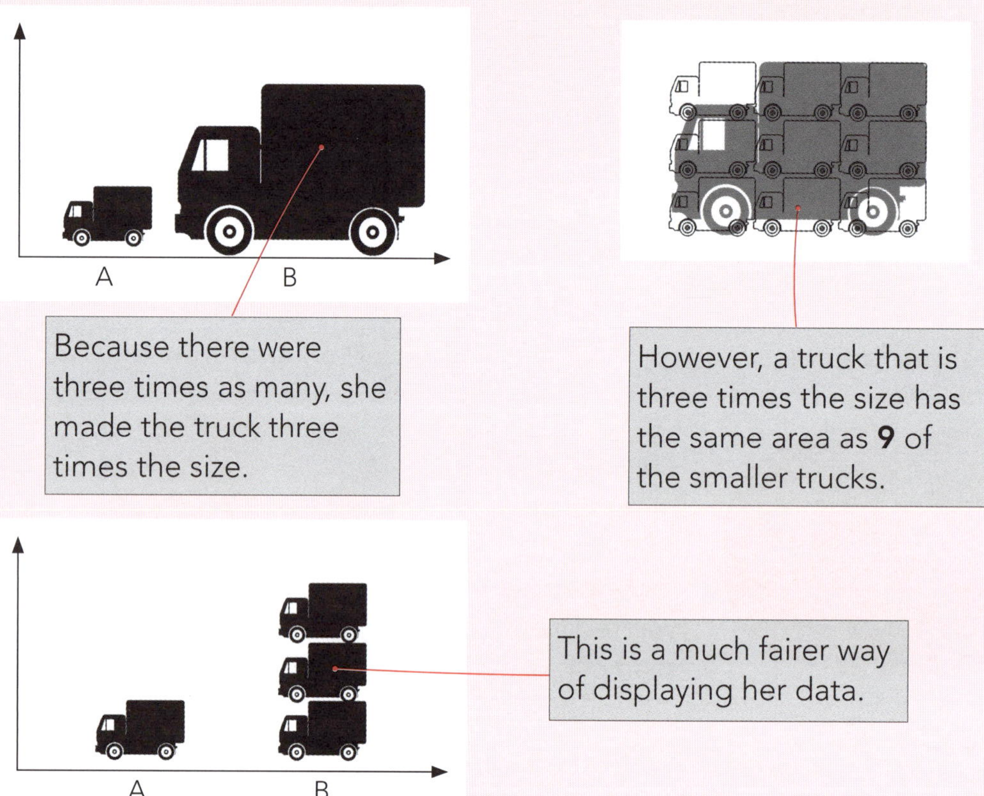

These are misleading because **images that are scaled up look disproportionally larger than they should**.

3 Graphs with axes that don't start at zero

Wedding guests were asked which dessert they would like.

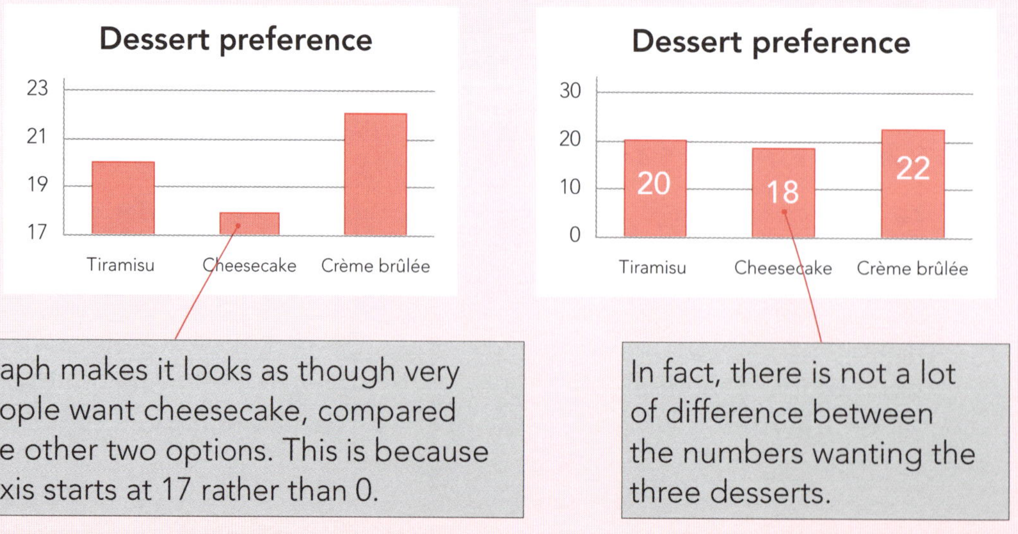

These are misleading because the **relative heights of points or bars are changed. This is very common.**

ISBN: 9780170451420

4 Pictographs with different-shaped or different-coloured images

This graph uses the heights of sports equipment to represent the number of spectators attending games.

Number of spectators

300

250

200

150

100

50

0

The area the basketball occupies makes it look as though many more people attended basketball compared with cricket.

In fact, cricket attracted the most spectators.

It looks as though the number of spectators watching softball is similar to cricket, but it's less than half.

These are misleading because **different shapes and colours can give a distorted impression of what they are representing**.

Describe what is misleading about these graphs.

1 A group of fishermen were asked which sort of rod fishing they preferred.

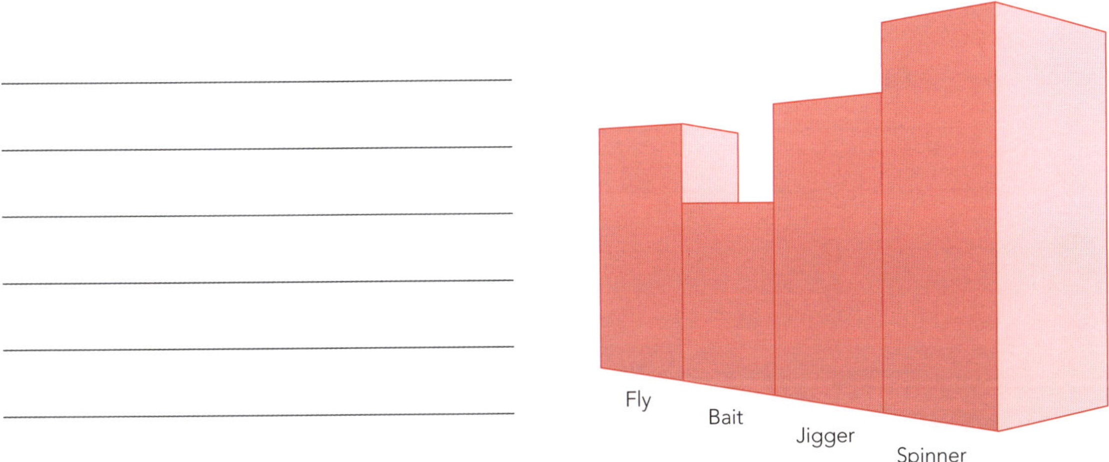

ISBN: 9780170451420

2 Students choose a piece of fruit from a platter. Each symbol represents one piece of fruit.

Fruit selected	
Banana	
Apple	
Strawberry	

3 Maia works in the local dairy. The graph shows the number of cartons of milk they sold on Monday and Tuesday.

4 Everybody in Year 9 was asked which they preferred out of pizza, hamburgers and pasta. The graph shows the results.

ISBN: 9780170451420

Data interpretation

- When interpreting graphs, you need to explain your reasoning.
- Sometimes there are several correct answers. This can lead to interesting discussion.

Answer the following questions.

1 The pie graph shows what Jeremy ate yesterday.

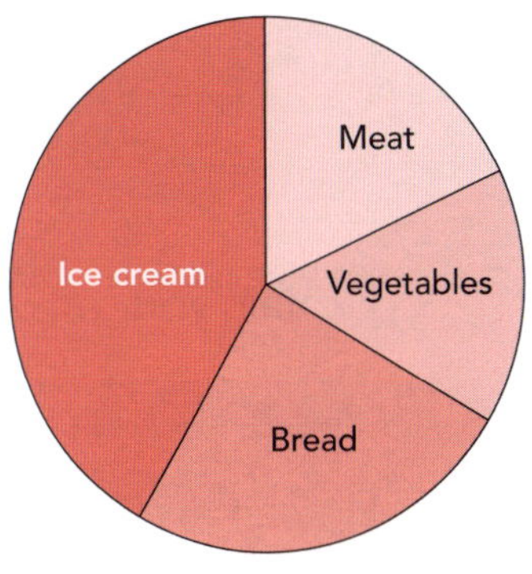

a Jeremy is a vegetarian.

☐ Agree ☐ Disagree ☐ Can't tell for sure

Explain your answer. ______________________________

____

b Jeremy has a healthy diet.

☐ Agree ☐ Disagree ☐ Can't tell for sure

Explain your answer. ______________________________

____

2 Ruth's younger brother spent Friday afternoon doing the activities below.

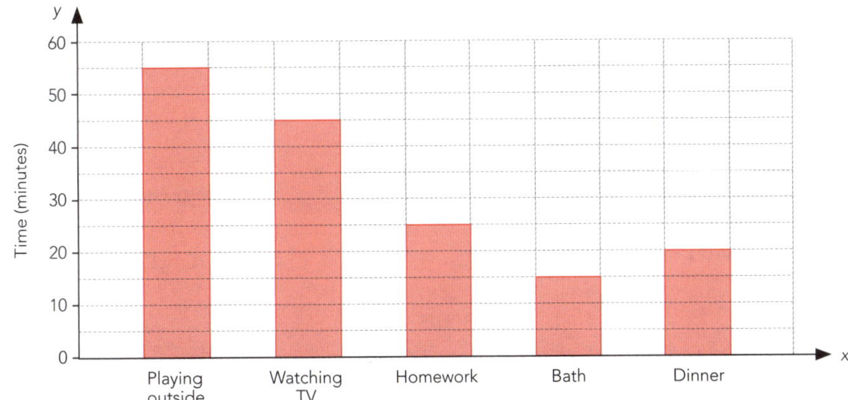

He spends most of his time playing outside.

☐ Agree ☐ Disagree ☐ Can't tell for sure

Explain your answer. ______________________________

____

ISBN: 9780170451420

3 Oscar counted the colours in his packet of lollies.

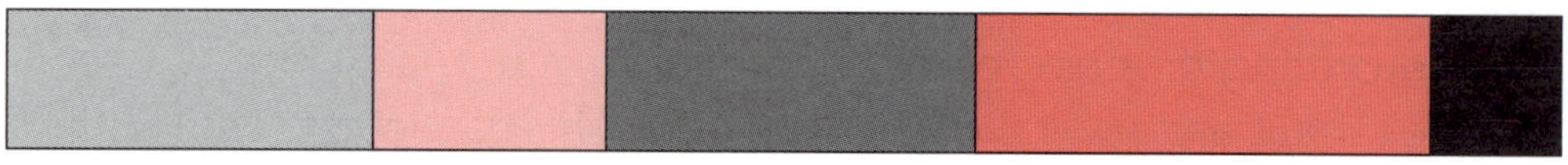

Red Orange Green Brown Blue

a He got twice as many brown lollies as orange ones.

☐ Agree ☐ Disagree ☐ Can't tell for sure

Explain your answer. ______________________________

____

b He can expect to get very few blue lollies in the next packet.

☐ Agree ☐ Disagree ☐ Can't tell for sure

Explain your answer. ______________________________

____

4 Kirsty made a spinner with eight equal divisions for a game. Each of the three players has a different-coloured counter. They use the spinner to decide who starts. Kirsty's friend says that the spinner is unfair.

☐ Agree ☐ Disagree

☐ Can't tell for sure

Explain your answer. ______________________________

____

____

____

Red Blue Green Red Blue Green Red Blue

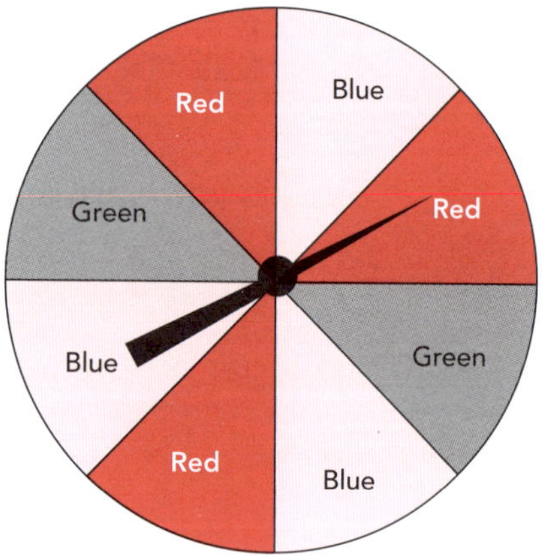

5 On Wednesday, students from 9D recorded their favourite biscuit flavours.
Most of 9D prefer chocolate biscuits.

☐ Agree ☐ Disagree

☐ Can't tell for sure

Flavour	**Tally**
Shortbread	||||
Chocolate	𝍸 𝍸 ||
Sultana	𝍸
Ginger	||

Explain your answer. ______________________________

____

____

____

ISBN: 9780170451420

6 Two friends compare how many hockey goals they have scored this season.

Burt

3	0	2
0	2	1
0	2	3

Ernie

1	1	3
2	2	0
0	1	1

Burt is a better player. ☐ Agree ☐ Disagree ☐ Can't tell for sure

Explain your answer. ______________________________

____

7 This pie graph shows how Stan spent his spare time yesterday. Today, Stan is more likely to read a book than to play outside in his spare time.

☐ Agree ☐ Disagree

☐ Can't tell for sure

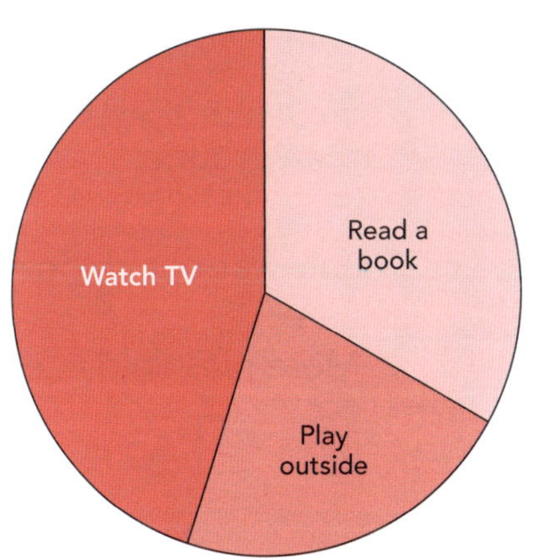

Explain your answer. ______________________________

____

____

____

8 This dot plot shows how members of a class got to school yesterday.

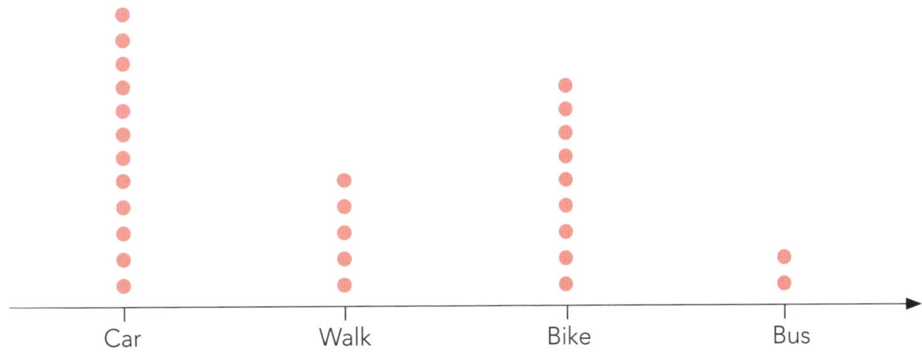

About a quarter of the class travelled to school by bike.

☐ Agree ☐ Disagree ☐ Can't tell for sure

Explain your answer. ______________________________

____

ISBN: 9780170451420

9 The number of pies sold by a market stall each month and average monthly temperatures were recorded.

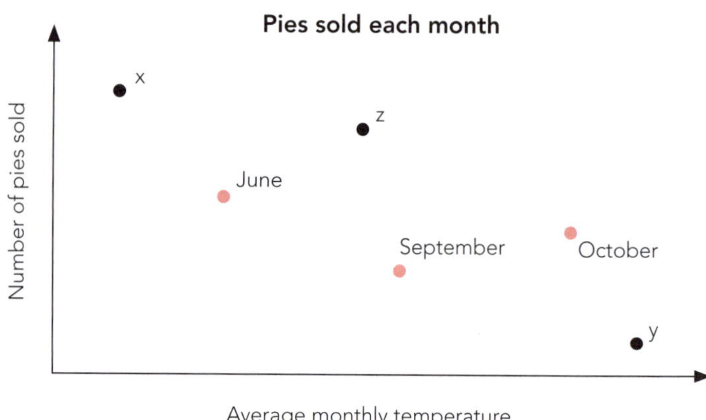

Match the months with the points on the graph.

a January was hotter than all other months and very few pies were sold. ________

b August was slightly cooler than September and more pies were sold than in June. ________

c July was the coldest month and lots of pies were sold ________

d More pies sold in cooler months.

☐ Agree ☐ Disagree ☐ Can't tell for sure

Explain your answer. ____

____

10 The graph shows the number of practices attended by members of the band.

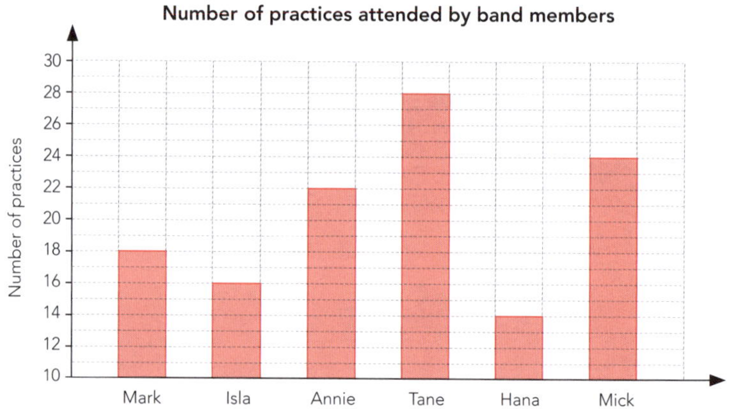

Are the following statements correct?

a Annie attended twice as many practices as Isla. Agree Disagree

b Tane attended twice as many practices as Hana. Agree Disagree

c This graph displays the data fairly. Agree Disagree

d Explain your answer for question **c**. ________________________________

____

 ISBN: 9780170451420

Revision 1

1 Select the best term to complete the sentence.

is extremely likely to	is guaranteed to	is likely to	is unlikely to	might

An event has a probability of 0.7, so it ______________________ occur.

2 Convert these probabilities into decimals and state which is more likely.

$\frac{1}{4}$ = ________ $\frac{4}{15}$ = ________ More likely: ________

3 Consider the spinner on the right.

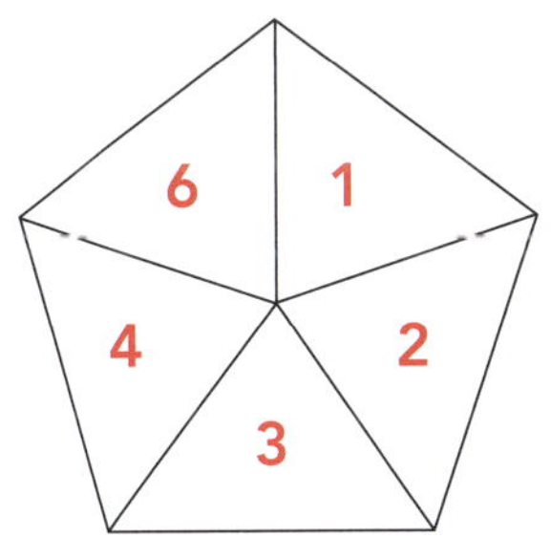

a List the outcomes from one spin (the sample space).

____

b The number of outcomes in the sample space = ______________

c Calculate the probability that it lands on a 6. P = ________

d Calculate the probability that it lands on an even number. P = ________

4 The probability of winning a game is 0.35. The probability of a draw = 0.1.

So therefore the probability of losing the game = ______________.

5 Helen threw a die 10 times. These were her results:

1 4 4 2 5 3 6 6 6 6

The probability that her eleventh throw is a 6 is:

☐ less than $\frac{1}{6}$ ☐ exactly $\frac{1}{6}$ ☐ more than $\frac{1}{6}$

6 Give an example of a descriptive variable. ______________________________

7 The weight of a packet of flour is an example of a ______________ variable.

8 In a survey, the students who bike to school were asked if they would like a change in the canteen menu.
This survey is likely to lead to a biased/unbiased result.

Explain your answer. ______________________________

____

ISBN: 9780170451420

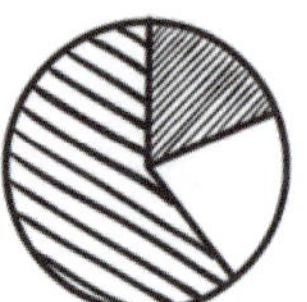

9 Which type(s) of data can be used in a pie graph?

☐ Descriptive ☐ Discrete ☐ Continuous

10 Members of a class were asked how they got to school today.

a Complete the table.

How did you get to school today?	Tally	Frequency
	III	
		9
		6
	卌 卌 I	
	Total	

b What is the probability that a student biked to school? __________

c What is the probability that a student arrived by motorised transport? __________

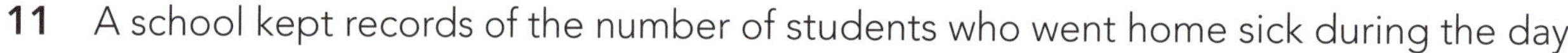

11 A school kept records of the number of students who went home sick during the day.

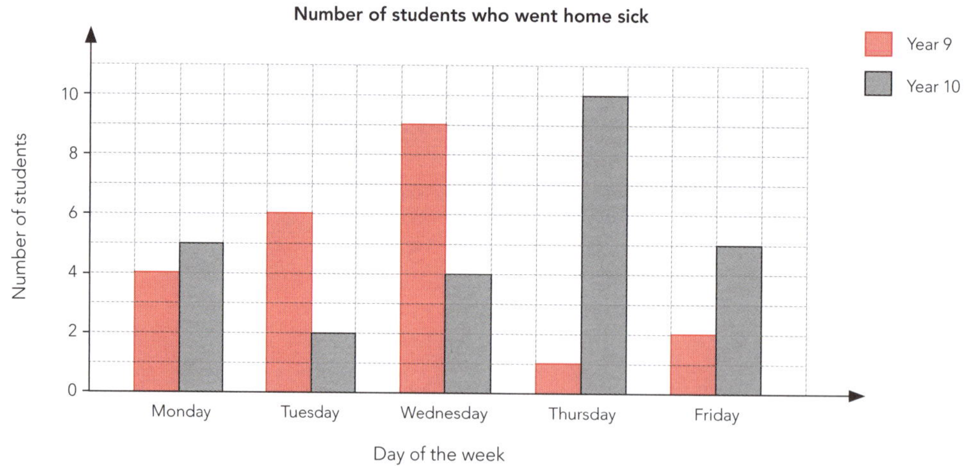

a How many students went home sick on Tuesday? __________

b Which day had the smallest number of students go home sick? __________

c More Year 9 students go home sick than Year 10 students.

☐ Agree ☐ Disagree ☐ Can't tell for sure

Explain your answer. ______________________________

____

ISBN: 9780170451420

12 Students were asked how many movies they watched in the weekend.

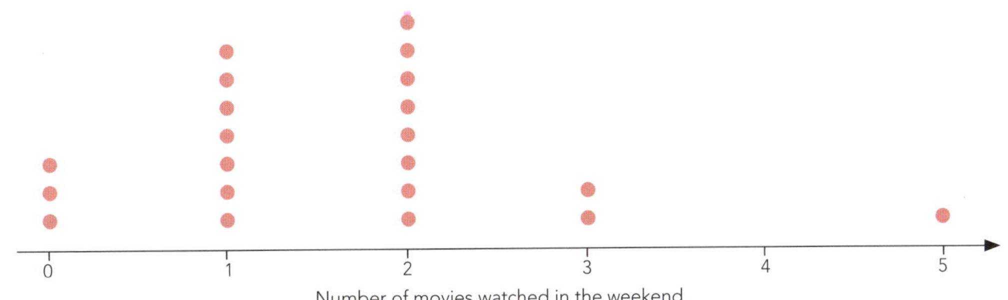

a How many students watched only one movie? ____________

b Describe any unusual features in this graph.

____

c Most students watched at least two movies.

☐ Agree ☐ Disagree ☐ Can't tell for sure

Explain your answer.

____

____

13 Calculate the mean, median, mode and range of this data set:

1 1 2 2 5 7 8 9 10 11 16 16 17

Mode = ______ Median = ______ Mean = ______ Range = ______

14 A survey was done on the total numbers of pets owned by members of the class.

Pet ownership

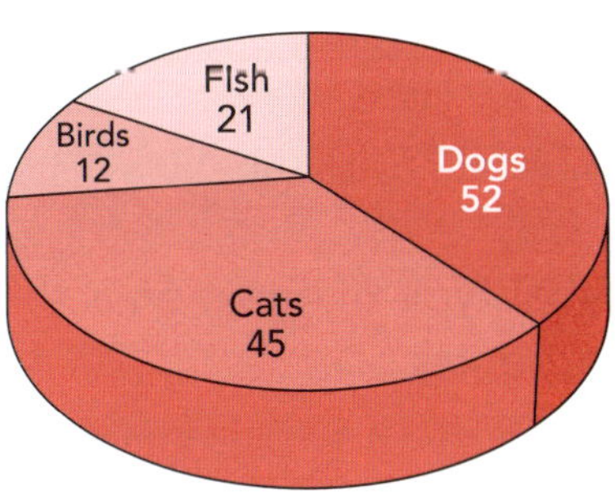

a How many birds did class members have? ____________

b How many pets were there altogether? ____________

c The graph appears to show cats are the most common pet. Is this correct?

☐ Yes ☐ No

Explain your answer. ____

____

ISBN: 9780170451420

Revision 2

1 Select the best term to complete the sentence.

an even chance	no chance	a small chance	a good chance

An event has a probability of 0.2, so it has ______________________ of occurring.

2 Convert these probabilities into decimals and state which is more likely.

69% = ________ $\frac{11}{16}$ = ________ More likely: ________

3 A coin is tossed and then a die is thrown.

a Complete the table to show all the possible outcomes.

		2				
H						

b Use the table to calculate the following probabilities.

i The probability of getting a tail and a 1. P = ________

ii The probability of getting a head and an even number. P = ________

4 Give an example of a continuous variable. ______________________

5 Your favourite takeaway is an example of a ______________________ variable.

6 What type of question is this? Do Year 9 students read more books than Year 10 students?

☐ Summary ☐ Comparative ☐ Relationship

7 Who should be Paradise High School's head student next year?

To find the answer, the school should: ☐ do a census ☐ take a sample

8 Which type(s) of data can be used in a histogram?

☐ Descriptive ☐ Discrete ☐ Continuous

 ISBN: 9780170451420

9 Data on students' eye colour was collected.

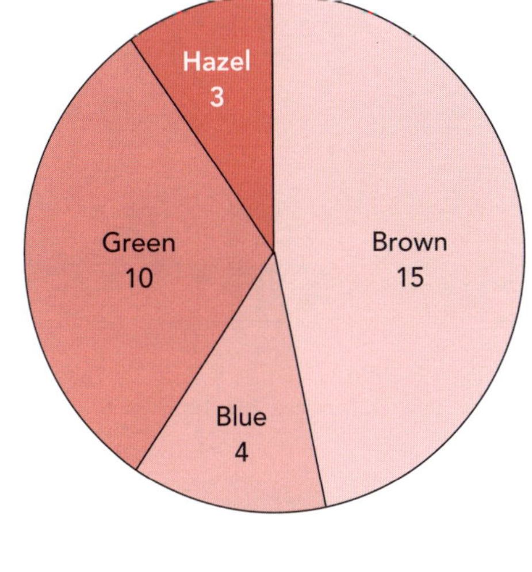

a How many students have green eyes? ____________

b How many students were surveyed? ____________

c Calculate the probability that a student did not have green eyes. ____________

d Most of the students have brown eyes.

Explain your answer. ____

____

10 A teacher recorded the time students took to complete a mathematics test.

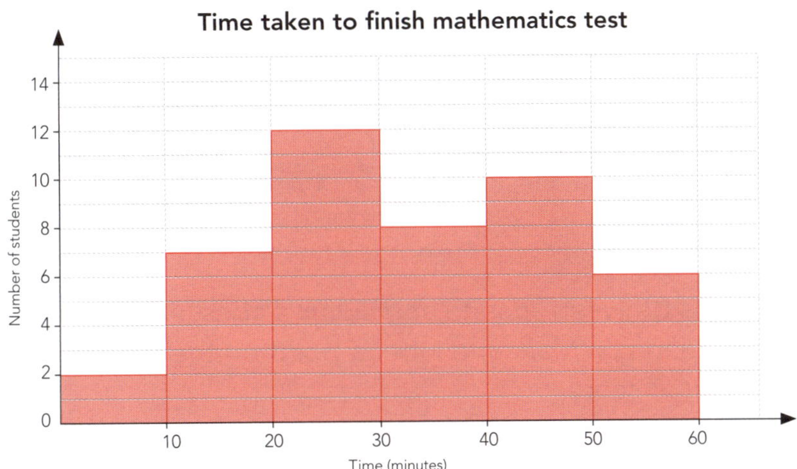

a What was the most common time taken? ____________

b How many took between 40 and 60 minutes? ____________

c Two students gave up.

☐ Agree ☐ Disagree ☐ Can't tell for sure

Explain your answer. ____

____

11 Calculate the mean, median, mode and range for this data set:

15 18 16 23 9 17 11 18 ____________________________

Mode = ________ Median = ________ Mean = ________ Range = ________

ISBN: 9780170451420

12 Quiz scores were plotted against age of a group of people.

a Who got the highest score? ____________

b Who was older than Tia but scored more in the quiz? ____________

c The quiz was harder for older people.

☐ Agree ☐ Disagree ☐ Can't tell for sure

Explain your answer. ______________________________

____

d Paul's age is between Juanita and Justin's ages, and his score was between Tia's and Brianna's. Mark and label a point on the graph that could represent Paul's age and score.

13 Students were asked what end-of-year outing they would prefer.

a How many students wanted to go mountain biking? ____________

b What fraction of the students wanted to go to the zoo?

____

c This graph displays the data well.

☐ Agree ☐ Disagree

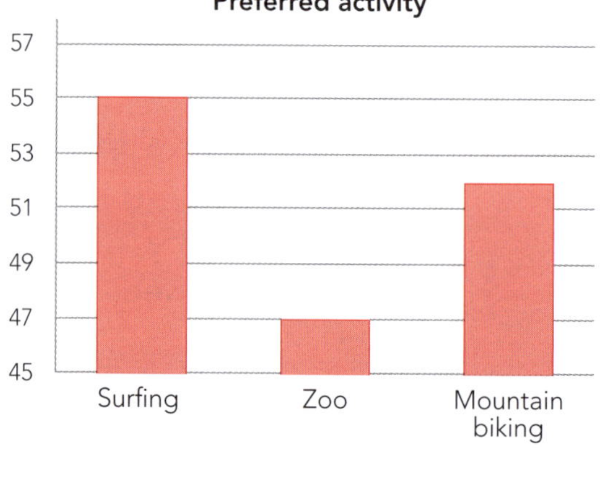

Explain your answer. ______________________________

____

ISBN: 9780170451420

Answers

Probability (pp. 6–21)

Fraction, decimal and percentage revision (p. 6)

Shaded circle picture	Fraction	Decimal	Percentage
	$\frac{3}{4}$	0.75	75%
	$\frac{2}{3}$	$0.\dot{6}$	$0.6\dot{6}\%$
	$\frac{1}{8}$	0.125	12.5%
	$\frac{2}{5}$	0.4	40%
	$\frac{3}{8}$	0.375	37.5%
	$\frac{5}{6}$	$0.8\dot{3}$	$0.8\dot{3}\%$
	$\frac{2}{6} = \frac{1}{3}$	$0.\dot{3}$	$33.\dot{3}\%$

The probability scale (p. 7)

1 1 certain, a sure thing, definite, guaranteed
0.9 very likely, almost certain
0.7 probable, good chance, likely
0.5 maybe, even chance, fifty-fifty
0.3 unlikely, maybe
0.1 slight chance, very unlikely
0 impossible, no chance, no way

Sample space (pp. 8–10)

1 a

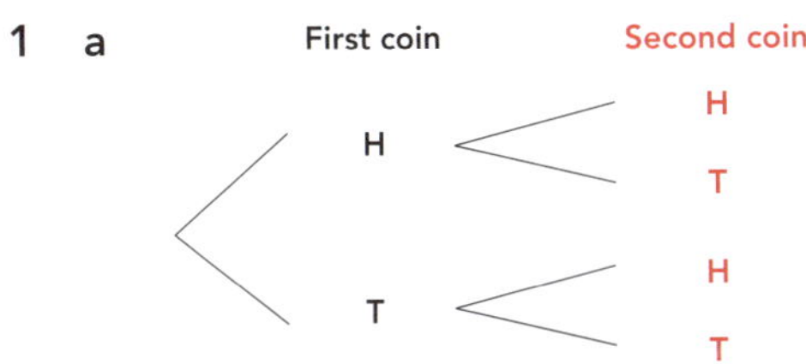

List the outcomes in the sample space:
HH, HT, TH, TT
The number of outcomes in the sample space
is **4**.

b

	H	T
H	HH	HT
T	TH	TT

Same result? ✓

c Number of outcomes for the first coin = **2**
Number of outcomes for the second coin = **2**
Multiplying these numbers gives **4**
Same result? ✓

2 a

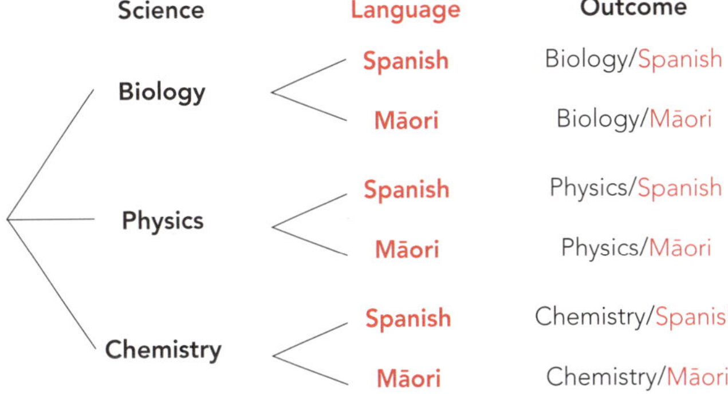

b The number of outcomes in the sample space is **6**.

c

	Spanish	Māori
Biology	Biology/Spanish	Biology/Māori
Physics	Physics/ Spanish	Physics/Māori
Chemistry	Chemistry/ Spanish	Chemistry/ Māori

Same result? ✓

d number of sciences x number of languages
= 3 x 2
= 6
Same result? ✓

ISBN: 9780170451420

Calculating theoretical probability (pp. 11–15)

1 **a** 1, 2, 3, 4, 5, 6 **b** 6

c $P = \frac{1}{6}$ **d** $P = \frac{2}{6} = \frac{1}{3}$

e $P = \frac{3}{6} = \frac{1}{2}$ **f** $P = 0$

g $P = \frac{6}{6} = 1$

2 **a** black marble, red marble, white marble

b 3 **c** $P = \frac{1}{3}$

d $P = \frac{2}{3}$ **e** $P = \frac{2}{3}$

f $P = 0$ **g** $P = \frac{6}{6} = 1$

3 **a**

First coin	Second coin	Outcomes
H	H	HH
	T	HT
T	H	TH
	T	TT

$P(HH) = \frac{1}{4}$

b

	H	T
H	HH	HT
T	TH	TT

$P(TH \text{ or } HT) = \frac{2}{4} = \frac{1}{2}$

c **i** $P(\text{no heads}) = \frac{1}{4}$

ii $P(\text{one or two heads}) = \frac{3}{4}$

iii They add to 1.
Reason: You have to get either no heads, one head or two heads.

iv Because there is only one way of getting TT or HH, but there are two ways of getting one of each — TH and HT.

4 **a**

Coin	Die: 1	2	3	4	5	6
H	H1	H2	H3	H4	H5	H6
T	T1	T2	T3	T4	T5	T6

b **i** $P = \frac{1}{12}$ **ii** $P = \frac{2}{12} = \frac{1}{6}$

iii $P = \frac{6}{12} = \frac{1}{2}$ **iv** $P = \frac{3}{12} = \frac{1}{4}$

v $P = 0$

5 **a**

Spinner	Die: 1	2	3	4	5	6
1	2	3	4	5	6	7
3	4	5	6	7	8	9
5	6	7	8	9	10	11

b **i** $P = \frac{1}{18}$ **ii** $P = \frac{3}{18} = \frac{1}{6}$

iii $P = 0$ **iv** $P = \frac{9}{18} = \frac{1}{2}$

Calculating probabilities based on surveys (pp. 16–17)

1 **a** 40

b $P(\text{pass}) = \frac{25}{40} = 0.625$

2 **a** $P(\text{hokey pokey}) = \frac{10}{25} = 0.4$

b $P(\text{hokey pokey or chocolate}) = \frac{10 + 8}{25} = 0.72$

3 **a** 60

b $P(\text{Samoan}) = \frac{15}{60} = 0.25$

c $P(\text{French or Japanese}) = \frac{24}{60} = 0.4$

d 81.67% (2 dp)

4 **a** 10

b $P(\text{win}) = \frac{3}{10} = 0.3$

c $P(\text{draw or lose}) = \frac{7}{10} = 0.7$

5 **a**

Year	Activity: Kayaking	Orienteering	Totals
Year 9	15	12	27
Year 10	20	13	33
Totals	35	25	60

b $P(\text{kayaking}) = \frac{35}{60} = 0.58$ (2 dp)

c $P(\text{Year 10}) = \frac{33}{60} = 0.55$

d $P(\text{Year 9 and orienteering}) = \frac{12}{60} = 0.2$

e 60.6% (1 dp)

Experimental probability (pp. 18–19)

1 **a** 5

b No
Because he did only 10 tosses. It might just have been chance that he got 6 tails.

c He needs to toss the coin lots of times.

 ISBN: 9780170451420

d

		Total	Probability	
Heads	𝍸𝍸𝍸𝍸𝍸 II	27	$\frac{27}{50}$	0.54
Tails	𝍸𝍸𝍸𝍸 III	23	$\frac{23}{50}$	0.46

e No
One hundred tosses is better than 10 tosses, but it still might just have been chance that he got 23 tails.

f

	Total	Probability (4 dp)	
Heads	708	$\frac{708}{1400}$	0.5057
Tails	692	$\frac{692}{1400}$	0.4943

g No.
Because although there were a lot more tosses, there is not much difference between 0.5057 and 0.4943.

h

Number of tosses	**10**	**50**	**1400**
P(Head)	0.4	0.54	0.5057
P(Tail)	0.6	0.46	0.4943

As the number of tosses increased, the probabilities got closer to 0.5.

i Very close to 500 000.

j No
What Andy has thrown before can have no effect on whether he gets heads or tails.

Complementary events (p. 20)

1 The probability that it won't rain = 0.7.

2 P(not throwing a 6) = $\frac{5}{6}$

3 P = 1 – 0.36 – 0.20 = 0.44

4 P(student didn't have a cat) = $\frac{16}{25}$ = 0.64

Comparing probabilities (p. 21)

1 $\frac{1}{4} = 0.25$ $\frac{1}{5} = 0.2$

More likely: $\frac{1}{4}$

2 $\frac{4}{5} = 0.8$ 79% = 0.79

More likely: $\frac{4}{5}$

3 85% = 0.85 $\frac{7}{8} = 0.875$

More likely: $\frac{7}{8}$

4 65% = 0.65 $\frac{3}{5} = 0.6$

More likely: 65%

5 $\frac{1}{8} = 0.125$ 10% = 0.1

More likely: $\frac{1}{8}$

6 $\frac{3}{8} = 0.375$ $\frac{1}{3} = 0.\dot{3}$

More likely: $\frac{3}{8}$

7 a $\frac{3}{9} = \frac{1}{3} = 0.\dot{3}$ b $\frac{2}{5} = 0.4$

c Bag B
Because the probability of getting a red marble is higher (0.4) for bag B.

Statistical concepts (pp. 22–24)

Census and sample (p. 22)

1	Sample	Answer doesn't matter very much. It would be difficult and very expensive to get answers from everybody in the North Island.
2	Census	Small population, so relatively easy to ask everybody.
3	Sample	Answer doesn't matter very much. It would be difficult and very expensive to get answers from the entire New Zealand high school population.
4	Census	Although expensive to find answers, the answer to the question is very important.

Types of variables (p. 23)

1	Descriptive	**2**	Continuous
3	Discrete	**4**	Continuous
5	C, D	**6**	A, E
7	B, F		

Investigative questions (p. 24)

1	Summary	**2**	Comparative
3	Comparative	**4**	Summary
5	Relationship	**6**	Summary
7	Relationship	**8**	Comparative

Data display (pp. 25–70)

1	Line graph/time series	**2**	Pie chart
3	Dot plot	**4**	Bar graph
5	Strip graph	**6**	Histogram
7	Tally chart	**8**	Scatter plot
9	Pictograph		

Tally charts and frequency tables (pp. 26–29)

1 a

Dinner choice	Tally	Frequency
Spaghetti	𝍸 |	6
Pizza	𝍸 𝍸 ||	12
Burrito	||||	4
Steak	𝍸 |||	8
	Total	**30**

b 30 **c** Pizza

d $P = \frac{6}{30} = 0.2$

2 a

Favourite emoticon	Tally	Frequency
	𝍸 𝍸 |	11
		0
	𝍸 ||	7
	𝍸	5
	||	2
	Total	**25**

b **c** $P = \frac{2}{25} = 0.08$

3 a Bike **b** 9

d $P = \frac{3}{12} = 0.25$

4 a

Item	Tally	Frequency
	𝍸 𝍸 |	11
	𝍸	5
	𝍸 𝍸 ||	12
	|	1
	|	1
	Total	**30**

b Cat **c** 29

d $P = \frac{12}{30} = 0.4$

Pictographs (pp. 30–32)

1 a 25 **b** 13

c $P = \frac{19}{25} = 0.76$

2 a Friday **b** 84

c $\frac{33}{84}$

3

Feeling	
Love it	☺ ☺ ☺ ☺ ☺ ☺
It's okay	😐 😐 😐 😐 😐 😐 😐 😐 😐
Dislike it	☹ ☹ ☹ ☹ ☹

a Descriptive **b** 15

c $P = \frac{5}{20} = 0.25$

Pie graphs (pp. 33–36)

1 a White **b** Red

c Silver **d** $\frac{43}{206}$

2 a 4 **b** 8

c 40 **d** 0.3

3 a 20 **b** 15

c 0.625 **d** 0.875

4

Type	Frequency	Sectors
Walk	9	3
Bike	3	1
Car	3	1
Bus	6	2
Scooter	3	1
Total	**24**	**8**

ISBN: 9780170451420

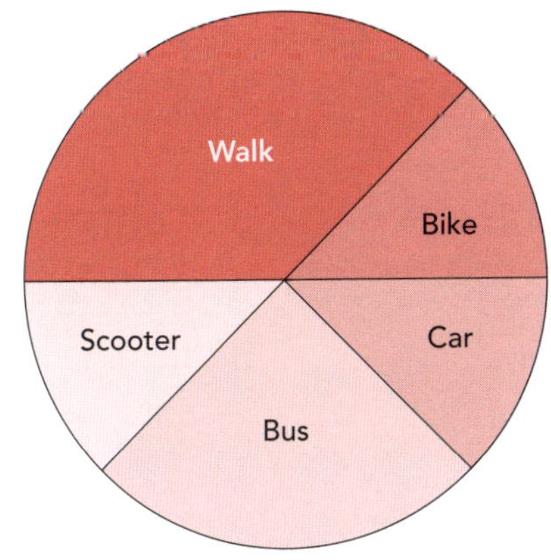

5

Type	Frequency	Sectors
Salt and vinegar	15	5
Ready salted	3	1
Sour cream and chives	12	4
Chicken	3	1
Other	3	1
Total	**36**	**12**

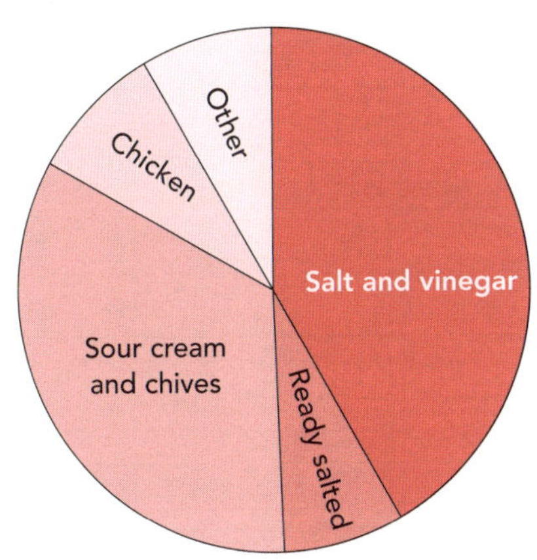

6

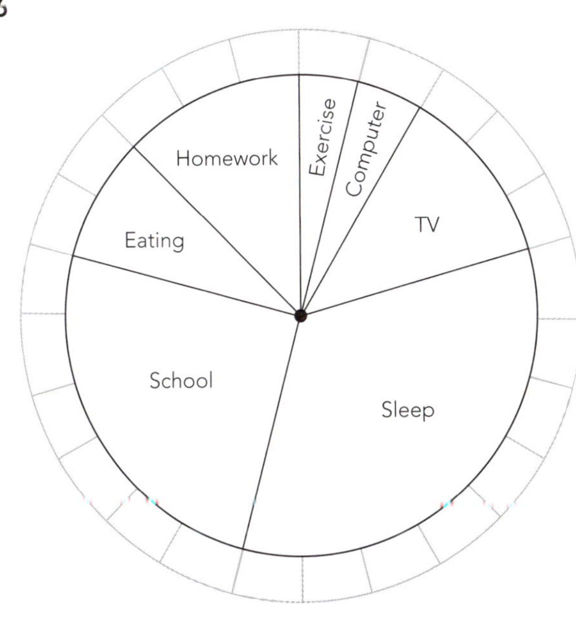

Strip graphs (pp. 37–39)

1 a 16 b 12
c $\frac{3}{16} = 0.1875$

2 a 20 b 70
c $\frac{5}{14} = 0.3571$

3 a Reuben b \$50
c \$250

4 a 2 kg b 8 kg
c Her **clothing** had twice as much mass as her **food**.

5

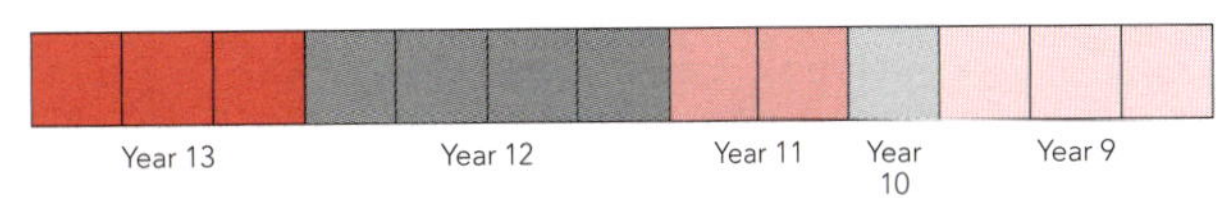

6

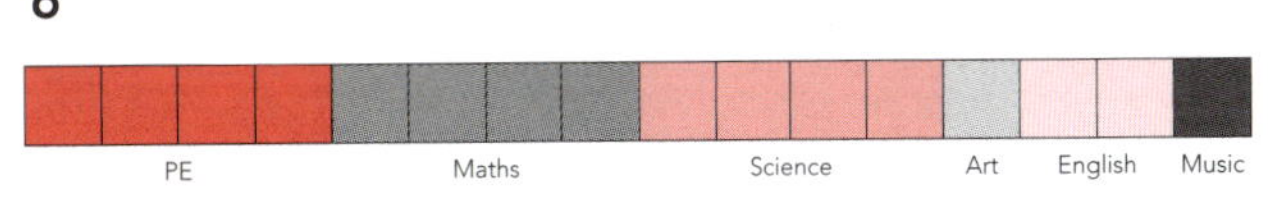

Reading axes (pp. 40–41)

1 Major 5 Minor 1
2 Major 50 Minor 25
3 Major 3 Minor 1
4 Major 10 Minor 2

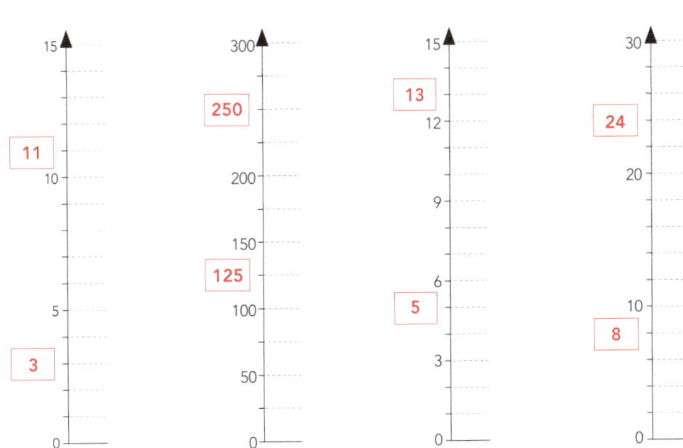

5 Major 4 Minor 2

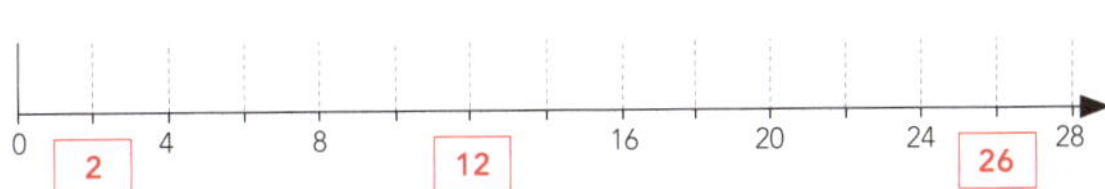

6 Major 1 Minor 0.2

Bar graphs (pp. 42–46)

1 a 15 b 30
c 78 d $\frac{15}{78}$
e 34.6%

2 a 4 b 14
c $\frac{5}{14}$

ISBN: 9780170451420

3 **a** Year 9 **b** Monday
c Year 10 with 1 more.

4

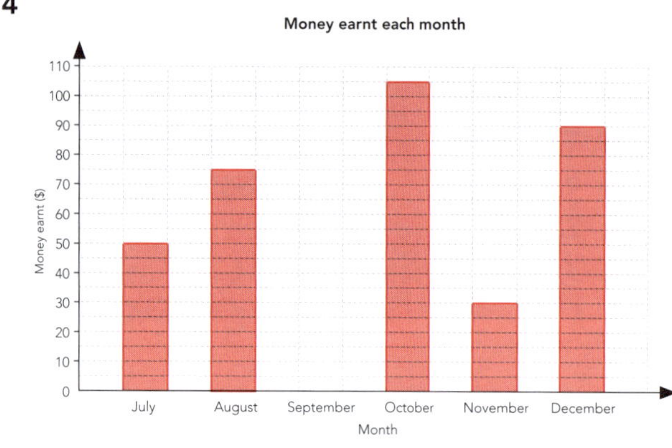

5

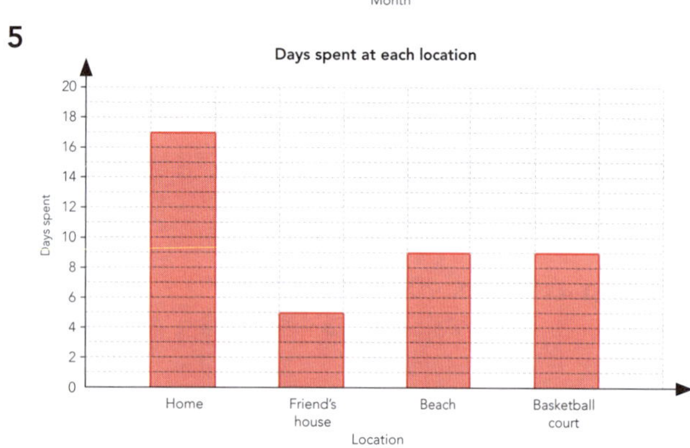

Line graphs (pp. 47–50)

1 **a** 17 **b** Thursday
c 104

2 **a** Week 2 **b** Year 9; 4 more
c Year 9. They had more absences in every week except week 2, when they had only 2 fewer.
Or: Year 10. Which had 81, while Year 9 had 66.

3

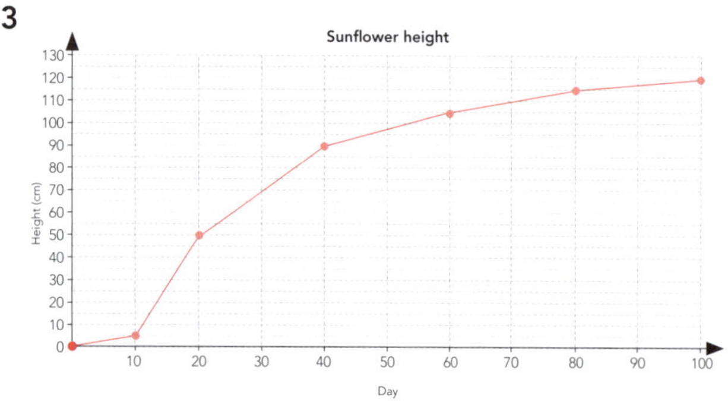

4

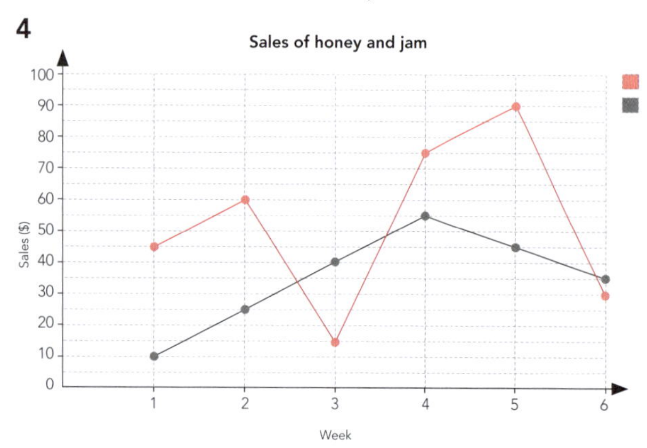

Histograms (pp. 51–54)

1 **a** 22 students **b** 24 students
c $\frac{7}{67}$

2 **a** 2–4 kg **b** 7 students
c 3 students **d** $\frac{7}{35} = 0.2$

3 **a** 2 days **b** 10–15°C
c 5 days **d** $\frac{24}{31}$

4

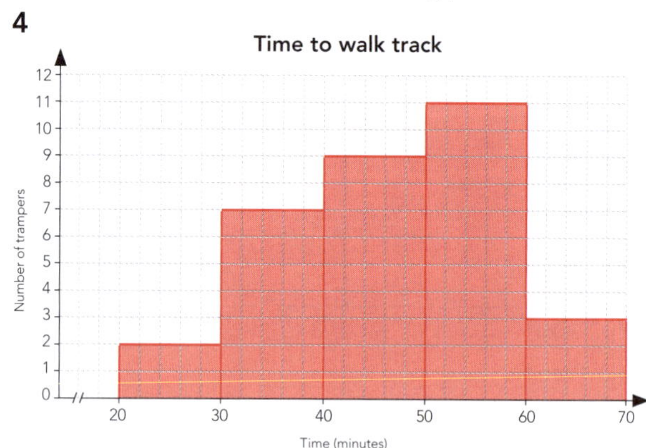

5

Minutes	Tally	Frequency
0–	卌	5
10–	卌 |	6
20–	||||	4
30–	||	2
40–	|||	3
50–	|	1
60–(70)	|	1
	Total	22

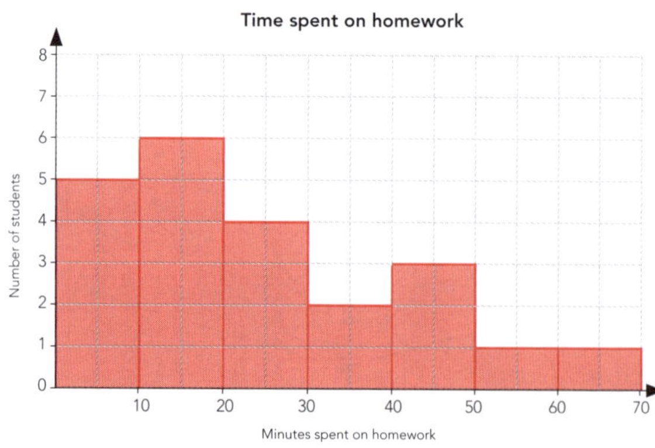

Dot plots (pp. 55–58)

1 **a** 1 hour **b** 6 students
c 21 **d** $\frac{5}{21}$

2 **a** Science
b There are more dots to the right of the Science graph, while most of the dots of the Mathematics graph are nearer the left.
c 25

ISBN: 9780170451420

3 a

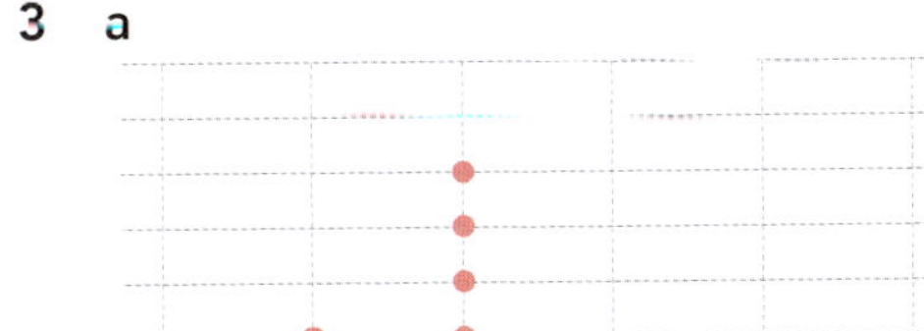

b $\frac{3}{18} = \frac{1}{6}$ c $\frac{9}{18} = 0.5$

4 a

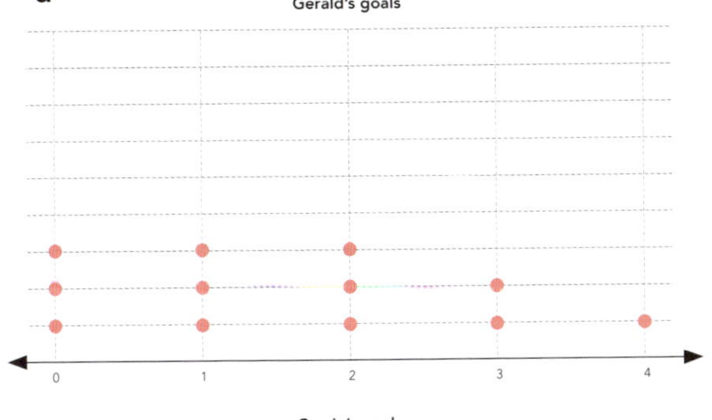

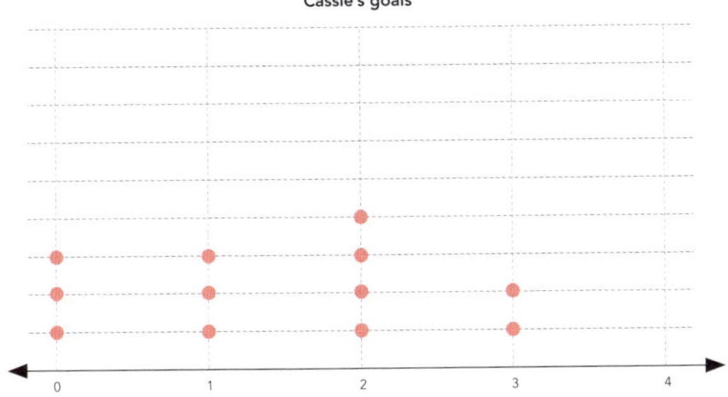

b Either: Agree, because Gerald scored more goals.
Or: Can't tell for sure, because we don't know what positions they were playing. Forwards have many more opportunities to score goals than backs.

Scatter plots (pp. 59–63)

1

Student	Coordinates	Description
a	(**9**, **240**)	They worked for **9** hours and earnt $**240**.
b	(**4**, **200**)	They worked for **4** hours and earnt $**200**.
c	(**6**, **150**)	They worked for **6** hours and earnt $**150**.

d 12 hours e 2 hours
f $140

2 a True b True
c False d False

3

Student	Coordinates	Description
a	(**22**, **4.6**)	They travelled **22** km and their bag was **4.6** kg.
b	(**15**, **4.3**)	They travelled **15** km and their bag was **4.3** kg.

c and d

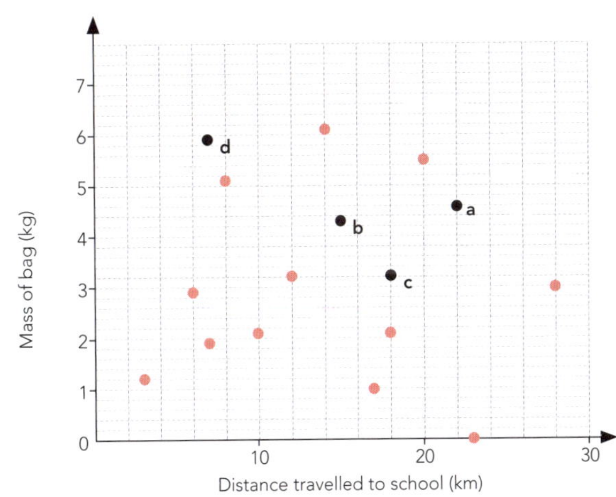

e 23 km f 3 kg

4

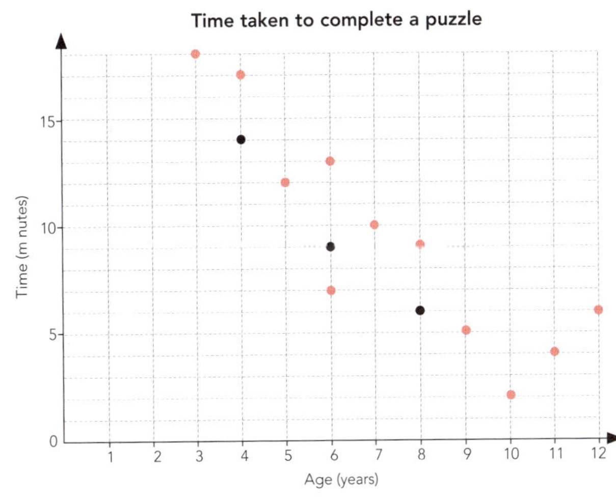

5 a x b z
c y

ISBN: 9780170451420

Data analysis (pp. 64–70)

Measures of centre (averages) (pp. 64–67)

1 **a** Mean $= \dfrac{4+5+1+9+8+2+6+7+8+5}{10} = 5.5$

b Mean $= \dfrac{6+6+4+2+7+9+2+1+6+7+3+12}{5}$

$= 5$

c Mean $= \dfrac{13+17+13+15+19+24+21+9+17+18+20}{11}$

$= 16.91$ or 16.9 (1 dp)

d Mean $= \dfrac{36+92+41+54+68+35+91+34+86+82+100+40}{12}$

$= 63.25$ or 63.3 (1 dp)

2 **a** Median = 2 **b** Median = 15
c Median = 7.5 **d** Median = 14

3 **a** 1, 3, 4, 4, 4, 6, 7, 8, 8, 9 Median = 5
b 2, 3, 3, 7, 7, 7, 10, 12 Median = 7
c 1, 3, 4, 4, 5, 8, 9, 10 Median = 4.5
d 12, 15, 21, 23, 23, 28, 35 Median = 23

4 **a** 2 **b** 1
c 3.5

5 **a** 4 **b** 10
c 14 and 21 **d** No mode
e No mode

6 **a** 0 **b** 0 and 5

Measure of spread — range (p. 68)

1 **a** 8 **b** 70

2 **a** Smallest number = 3
b Biggest number = 79

3 9C: Range = 8
9D: Range = 5
9C has a larger range (8) than 9D (5), so the test results for 9C are more variable.

Unusual features (pp. 69–70)

1

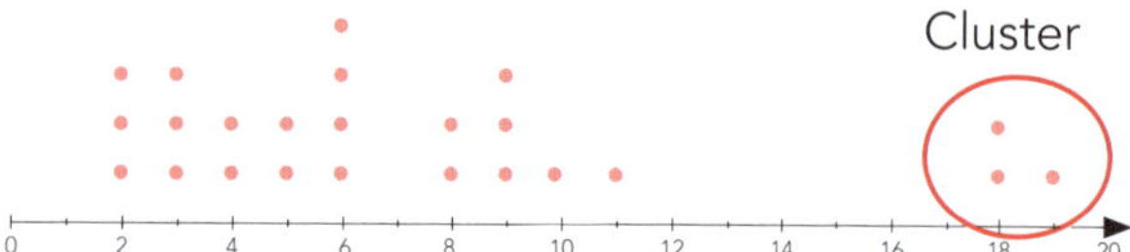

2

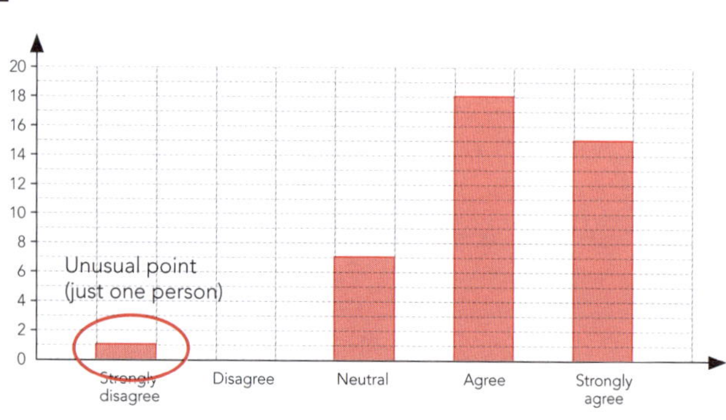

3

Cluster
Unusual point

4 A mark of 3 is an unusual point because all the other marks were 10 or more.

5 Nine siblings is an unusual point because all other families had 4 or fewer.

Statistical literacy (pp. 71–80)

Sampling and bias (pp. 71–72)

	Situation	Big enough sample?	Fair or biased?
1	Asking the first 5 students to get to class about whether they have completed their homework or not.	✗	Biased
	Why? Students who get to class on time are probably more likely to have done their homework.		
2	Surveying 50 Year 9 boys about what music they want at the disco.	✓	Biased
	Why? No girls asked. Girls are likely to want different music from boys. Asked only Year 9 students.		
3	Asking every tenth student on the Year 9 roll surveyed about what music they want at the disco.	✓	Fair
	Why? Every tenth student is unlikely to result in any one group being unfairly selected.		
4	Asking 30 students at the canteen if they want to see school ties made compulsory.	✓	Biased
	Why? Students at the canteen may not have the same view as those who don't buy their lunch from the canteen, and are unlikely to be 10% of school.		

Your answers may be different. If so, discuss them with your teacher.

5 Students who are sitting together are likely to have the same views.

6 Some people, especially the elderly, may not have cellphones, so are unavailable for the survey. Others are likely to be working in jobs where they are too busy or cannot answer their phones.

7 Some people, especially the elderly, may not have cellphones, or may not be familiar with texting. The people who bother to respond are likely to have strong views, so are unlikely to reflect the general population.

ISBN: 9780170451420

8 People in the mall are unlikely to reflect the views of the general population.
Many people avoid surveys in malls and only those with spare time are likely to respond.
9 Members of the netball team are probably more likely to want compulsory PE than those not in teams. Assuming it is a girls' netball team, their views are likely to be different from boys' views.

Recognising unfair data displays (pp. 73–76)

1 The graph makes it look as though the number of fishermen preferring spinners is far greater than any of the other groups because it is the closest, and you can see the 'side' of the bar.
2 The strawberries are bigger, more spread out and bolder images, so they catch the eye and look more popular than they should.
3 They sold twice as many cartons on Tuesday, but it looks as though they sold more than that because the carton is twice as wide and twice as tall.
4 The numbers represented on the graph are 87, 90 and 85. It looks as though the differences between them are much bigger than they really are because the graph does not start at 0.

Data interpretation (pp. 77–80)

You may have different answers and reasons. If so, discuss them with your teacher.

1 a Either: Disagree, because he ate meat yesterday.
Or: Can't tell for sure, because this may have been an occasion when he felt obliged to eat meat, whereas normally he wouldn't.
b Either: Disagree, because about a third of what he ate yesterday was ice cream, which is normally not regarded as very healthy food. Also, he didn't eat many vegetables.
Or: Can't tell for sure, because this may have been a special occasion when he ate food that was very different from what he would normally eat.
2 Either: Disagree, because on this day he only spent 55 minutes playing outside, whereas he spent 105 minutes doing other things.
Or: Can't tell for sure, because this is just one day. On other days the times he spends doing these activities might be quite different, especially if it's raining.
3 a Agree, because the strip representing brown lollies is twice as long as the one representing orange lollies.
b Either: Agree, because there were very few in this packet and other packets are likely to be similar.
Or: Can't tell for sure, because this is just one packet. The distribution of colours may vary between packets.
4 Agree, because there are three sectors for each of blue and red, but only two sectors for green, so the person with the green counter is less likely to start.
5 Either: Agree, because there were 12 who preferred chocolate and 11 who preferred other flavours.
Or: Can't tell for sure, because some students may have been absent, and it would take just one person who did not prefer chocolate to make the statement incorrect.
6 Either: Agree, because Burt scored 2 more goals than Ernie.
Or: Can't tell for sure, because we don't know what positions they play. Ernie might be a back with few opportunities to score goals, and he may have contributed by preventing the opposition form scoring goals.
7 Either: Agree, because he is most likely to follow the same pattern each day.
Or: Can't tell for sure, because it might be raining today. Or maybe he spent more time reading yesterday because he wanted to finish an exciting book.
8 Either: Disagree, because there are 28 students altogether and a quarter of 28 is 7. So more than a quarter travelled by bike.
Or: Can't tell for sure, because this may not have been a typical day. The numbers travelling by each method are likely to vary depending on the weather.
9 a y b z
c x
d Agree, because the most pies were sold in June, July and August when it is coldest, and the smallest number of pies were sold in September, October and January when it is warmer.
10 a Disagree b Agree
c Disagree
d The *y*-axis starts at 10, which makes the differences between the numbers of practices attended look more different than they really are.

ISBN: 9780170451420

Revision 1 (pp. 81–83)

1 An event has a probability of 0.7, so it **is likely to** occur.

2 $\frac{1}{4} = 0.25$ $\frac{4}{15} = 0.26$ More likely: $\frac{4}{15}$

3 **a** 1, 2, 3, 4, 6 **b** 5
c 0.2 **d** 0.6

4 0.55

5 exactly $\frac{1}{6}$

The probability of throwing any number between 1 and 6 on a fair die is always $\frac{1}{6}$, regardless of what has been thrown previously.

6 Any colour, name of something, etc.
Otherwise check with your teacher.

7 continuous

8 Biased, because those who bike to school are likely to have different opinions regarding canteen food than those who don't bike to school. They might be more likely to want a healthier option.

9 Descriptive

10 **a**

How did you get to school today?	Tally	Frequency
	|||	3
	卌 ||||	9
	卌 |	6
	卌 卌 |	11

b $\frac{3}{29}$ or 0.1034 **c** $\frac{17}{29}$ or 0.5862

11 **a** 8 **b** Friday
c Either: Disagree, because 22 Year 9 students went home sick compared with 26 Year 10 students.
Or: Can't tell for sure, because, while the statement is true for this particular week, it may not be true during most other weeks.

12 **a** Seven
b One student had watched five movies — at least two more than any other student.
c Agree, because 26 students watched two or more movies, compared with 22 students who watched zero or one movie.

13 Mode = No mode Median = 8
Mean = 8.08 Range = 16

14 **a** 12 **b** 130
c Yes, because that is the sector which looks closest, and also because you can see more of the side of the sector. In fact, the number of dogs (52) was greater than the number of cats (45).

Revision 2 (pp. 84–86)

1 An event has a probability of 0.2, so it has **a small chance** of occurring.

2 69% = 0.69 $\frac{11}{16} = 0.6875$ More likely: 69%

3 **a**

	1	2	3	4	5	6
H	H1	H2	H3	H4	H5	H6
T	T1	T2	T3	T4	T5	T6

b **i** $P = \frac{1}{12}$ or $0.08\dot{3}$
ii $P = \frac{3}{12}$ or $\frac{1}{4}$ or 0.25

4 Anything measured, e.g. length, weight, time, volume.
Otherwise check with your teacher.

5 descriptive 6 Comparative

7 do a census 8 Continuous

9 **a** 10 **b** 32
c $\frac{22}{32}$ or $\frac{11}{16}$ or 0.6875
d Disagree, because 15 out of 32 students had brown eyes, and that is less than half.

10 **a** Between 20 and 30 minutes
b 16 students
c Either: Agree, because 2 students spent less than 10 minutes doing the test.
Or: Can't tell for sure, because the 2 students who spent less than 10 minutes might have been extremely smart and finished it quickly, or they might have had to leave, e.g. for an appointment.

11 Mode = 18 Median = 16.5
Mean = 15.9 (1 dp) Range = 14

12 **a** Fatima **b** Brianna
c Either: Disagree, because there is no clear trend in the graph, with Brianna, who was older than most, getting a good score.
Or: Can't tell for sure, because there are only six points on the graph, and that is not enough evidence for making a general statement.
d

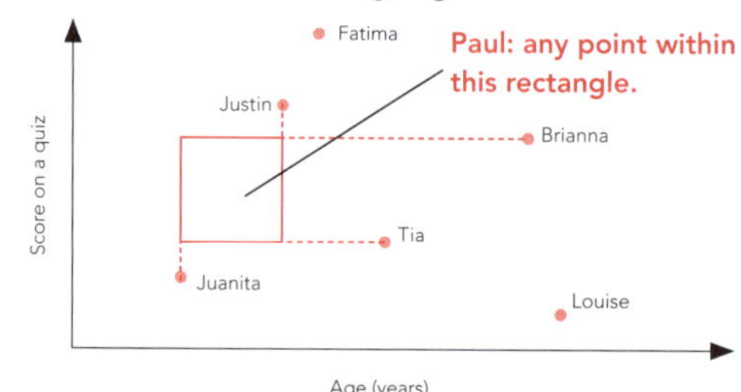

13 **a** 52 **b** $\frac{47}{154}$
c Disagree, because the *y*-axis does not start at zero, so it looks as though very few people want to go to the zoo compared with those who want to go surfing and mountain biking. However, nearly a third would like to go to the zoo.

ISBN: 9780170451420